THE
Relationships
Workbook for
BPD

Skills to Help You Cultivate
Emotional Safety, Deepen Understanding,
and Build Stronger Connections

DANIEL J. FOX, PhD

New Harbinger Publications, Inc.

Publisher's Note

NEW HARBINGER PUBLICATIONS is a registered trademark of New Harbinger Publications, Inc.

New Harbinger Publications is an employee-owned company.

Copyright © 2025 by Daniel J. Fox
New Harbinger Publications, Inc.
5720 Shattuck Avenue
Oakland, CA 94609
www.newharbinger.com

Cover design by Amy Daniel

Acquired by Elizabeth Hollis Hansen

Edited by Amber Williams

Library of Congress Cataloging-in-Publication Data on file

Printed in the United States of America

27   26   25

10   9   8   7   6   5   4   3   2   1   First Printing

"This compassionate, practical workbook is a much-needed guide for individuals with borderline personality disorder (BPD) who long for meaningful relationships but feel overwhelmed by fear, shame, or emotional volatility. Daniel J. Fox is a true expert on BPD, and his deep understanding of what maintains this disorder and how to shift these patterns is evident throughout. The exercises feel validating and empowering, and offer a clear path toward emotional safety and connection."

—**Liz Ross, PhD**, clinical psychologist, founder of the Coping Resource Center, assistant professor at Baylor College of Medicine, and past president of the Houston Psychological Association (HPA)

"*The Relationships Workbook for BPD* is a thoughtful, compassionate guide for those with BPD who struggle with relationship problem areas. Daniel J. Fox offers practical tools and exercises that build progressively toward developing healthier relationships. The inclusion of guidance and tools for loved ones make this workbook a unique resource for those who struggle with BPD and their support systems, and an incredible resource for graduate students and clinicians."

—**Diane Stoebner-May, PhD, ABPP**, clinical associate professor of psychology at Sam Houston State University

"To read a book filled with optimism and hope for those navigating relationships impacted by BPD is refreshing. Daniel J. Fox leads his readers through an insightful, honest, and challenging course of self-exploration. His expertise sets individuals on a path to clarity and success with their favorite people. With thought-provoking exercises, the reader is empowered to achieve stability and fulfillment in their relationships."

—**Tennille Warren-Phillips, PsyD**, founder of Relate Psychological Services, and chief psychologist at a pretrial detention facility

"Daniel Fox delivers a clear and actionable road map to developing healthier relationships. Grounded in evidence-based strategies and written with expertise, this workbook is an essential resource for anyone navigating the complexities of BPD. It's a valuable tool for anyone seeking greater stability, communication, and connection in their personal life."

—**Marshall Motsenbocker, PhD,** licensed psychologist

"This workbook empowers readers from page one! Daniel J. Fox brings honesty, compassion, and structure to the complex experience of navigating relationships in the context of BPD. With relatable storytelling and down-to-earth guidance, readers discover practical tools to build new skills, deepen self-understanding, and find resilience. Whether you're just starting or returning to this inner work, this workbook provides a safe and nonjudgmental space for meaningful change."

—**Nubia Angelina Mayorga, PhD**, clinical psychologist, and research fellow at Massachusetts General Hospital, Harvard Medical School

This book is dedicated to my three heartbeats:
my wife, Lydia, and my two children, Alexandra and Sebastian

Contents

BPD Relationship Workbook

Relationships are central catalysts to the progression or regression of growth in everyone, but especially for those with borderline personality disorder (BPD). The "Father of Borderline Personality Disorder," John G. Gunderson, MD, was instrumental in successfully identifying and treating individuals with borderline personality disorder (MacMillan 2019). One of his central concepts and questions is centered around *Is BPD a relationship disorder?* As a psychologist who has specialized in the identification and treatment of BPD for over twenty years, I can answer this question with a resounding, "absolutely." This workbook is part of my approach to identifying and working with individuals with BPD, but it also addresses relationship needs, wants, hopes, fears, and all those additional components that drive BPD symptoms and perpetuate what we're going to call BPD relationship problem areas.

My clients with BPD often tell me how much they value their relationships, but they feel suffocated by fear due to old wounds, negative beliefs, and perceptions of self and others. This loud and continuous internal dialogue influences how they see themselves, the important people in their life, and their relationships. This also contributes to the creation of their BPD relationship problem areas, which you'll identify in chapter 1. You've picked up this workbook because you want to learn how to turn down the volume of self-shame and hate, how to bolster healthy relationships, and how to see your life with that important person in a hopeful way. When I talk with partners of individuals with BPD, they often tell me that they want that person to be "ok," get better, be more in control, and stop hurting themselves and others. But few know that there's a pathway to achieving this and it's not hopeless for someone with BPD to manage their relationships and life better. You've taken a huge step by opening this workbook; being a willing participant is crucial to initiating change and growth.

BPD is a complex disorder that feels like it infects your core self. However, this does not mean that you *are* BPD, it means that you *have* BPD. The igniting forces are core content that drive your BPD maladaptive beliefs, behaviors, and patterns that we call surface content, and these impact your relationships in adverse ways through the development and perpetuation of your BPD relationship problem areas. But you can live and experience your life and relationships differently.

As you go through this workbook, you'll be supported and encouraged to continually envision the relationships you want. Hope is a central component of this and a powerful thing in treatment, in relationships, and in all parts of your life. This workbook will help you get on that path to more hopeful, clearer, stronger, and more stable relationships. Congratulations to those with BPD, their partners, friends, loved ones, and all those along for this journey for having the courage to get started.

Workbook and Life Perspective

Life is about probabilities, not guarantees, and this is true in relationships as well. For example, if you talk honestly, listen to each other, and try to work through problems calmly, there's a better chance your relationship will be strong and healthy. But if you ignore issues, act out, or don't listen, the probability of things going wrong is much higher. Engaging in adaptive behaviors doesn't guarantee a perfect outcome, but it increases the probability of positive outcomes, just like bad or maladaptive behavior increases the probability of problems, confusion, and relationship dissolution.

This framework is something I've used in my professional and personal life, and it's infused throughout the workbook. I want to encourage you to internalize this view, as I believe it'll motivate you to move forward and embrace adaptive behaviors over maladaptive ones. It's not always an easy choice, but in the long run, it leads to the healthiest outcome in my humble opinion.

Is This Workbook Only for Those in Romantic Relationships?

This workbook is designed to empower those with BPD as well as those who know, love, treat, and interact with them. This workbook isn't just for romantic partners, but all types of relationships. You can go through this workbook alone, or with your partner, child, family member, coworkers, clients, or patients, as this workbook is a non-pejorative tool to help you manage relationships and to help that other person in the relationship with you.

What makes this workbook different is that it isn't only aimed at helping you learn adaptive strategies to manage your maladaptive BPD relationship beliefs, behaviors, and patterns. It's also for that person, or persons, in your life, in a romantic relationship or not, who you want to feel closer to so you can have a more stable and honest connection with them.

This Workbook Can Be for More than Just You

Many behaviors, destructive or growth promoting, tend to be habits; addressing and changing them takes more than a single effort or single dose of insight. This workbook will help you learn and incorporate these skills going forward as it doesn't have just a singular function, but it uses a dual approach. This guide will give you helpful tips and strategies if you have BPD, but it'll also offer ways for you and the people in your life to understand each other better and feel closer. It's meant to help you connect more with the people you care about, and for them to feel more connected to you too.

Building and managing relationships can be tough, and having BPD can make it even harder. In this workbook, we're going to talk about the term "favorite person" (FP), which we'll use to describe someone who is very important to you in your life. This could be anyone: a romantic partner, family member, coworker, friend, or someone you really care about. An FP is a person you feel an extremely strong connection to, someone you often feel like is the center of your emotional world.

Being around them, or even just thinking about them, can really affect how you feel and how you see yourself, others, and situations. Your FP might be one or more people in your life who mean a lot to you, and they each offer something unique, but they all hold a special place in your life and heart. How they treat you and how you believe they see you can really impact your mood in negative and positive ways.

Throughout this workbook, there will be exercises, activities, and supportive strategies for you, but there is also online content for your FP to download so they can actively participate and support you along the way. These tools will help strengthen your relationship and lessen the adverse impact of your relationship problem areas due to the dual approach.

How This Workbook Is Organized

Below is a brief breakdown of each chapter, intended to enhance your insight into BPD and improve your relationships while living with BPD. It's broken into nine chapters, and each chapter builds on the last. You'll learn step by step how to spot patterns, understand what's really going on, and make lasting changes.

- Chapter 1 kicks things off by helping you spot ten common relationship problems that people with BPD often face. You'll figure out which ones are showing up in your own life. Each section in this chapter includes questions to help you dig deeper into how these problems started and why they're still happening. This chapter lays the foundation for everything that comes next.

- Chapter 2 teaches you the basics of BPD, what it is, and how it affects relationships. You'll also learn how to talk to your FP (favorite person) about BPD in a way that feels honest but not overwhelming. There are clear Q&As to help explain confusing parts, plus sections on how to ask for support and what to expect as you grow.

- Chapter 3 helps you learn what a healthy relationship actually looks like. You'll explore things like trust, communication, and how to share your emotional and physical needs. Each topic includes practice tips so you can build stronger habits. You'll also learn how to turn arguments into helpful conversations instead of blow-ups.

- Chapter 4 digs into relationship dynamics—how you act with others and how they act with you. This chapter helps you understand the different "roles" you and others take on in relationships, and how these roles affect closeness. You'll also look at protective behaviors that might be pushing people away without you realizing it.

- Chapter 5 focuses on how BPD can twist the way you see yourself and others. You'll learn how your self-image can shift quickly, and what to do to keep it steady. There's a section that helps you see your FP more clearly, and strategies to stop repeating unhealthy relationship cycles. Worksheets help you reflect and practice new ways of thinking.

- Chapter 6 is all about facing relationship insecurities. You'll explore fears around abandonment and closeness, and work on building more secure connections. This chapter helps you understand attachment styles and gives you tools to create the kind of relationship you want, based on trust, not neediness.

- Chapter 7 teaches you how to grow closer without losing yourself. You'll learn better communication skills, like how to express feelings without things getting off track. It includes specific tools, like the "sandwich technique," to help you share tough stuff more gently. There's also guidance on how to keep conversations steady, even when emotions run high.

- Chapter 8 helps you uncover how your past still affects you today. Many of our reactions in relationships come from old habits we picked up growing up. This chapter helps you spot those patterns, understand them, and make new choices. Activities and examples help you connect the dots between your past and your present behavior.

- Chapter 9 pulls everything together. You'll reflect on how far you've come, what's changed, and where you want to go. This chapter helps you strengthen your relationship with your FP, build healthy habits, and create a steady, supportive connection. It's a celebration of your growth and a guide to keeping it going.

This workbook is designed to go with you at your pace. You can move through it chapter by chapter or focus on the areas that feel most important right now. Either way, you'll come away with a better understanding of yourself and stronger tools for healthier relationships.

Throughout this workbook there will be many case examples, and you'll learn about their experiences, learning opportunities, and how they used the skills outlined in this workbook to better their relationships.

How to Maximize This Workbook

To get the most out of this workbook, you'll need to go back to the insights you learn and use them regularly to create more positive and hopeful perspectives. This will help you to keep growing personally and in your relationships by trying new, healthier behaviors and making them part of your everyday relationship habits.

What's the Pace for This Workbook?

This workbook lets you go at your own pace, so you can work on issues when you're ready and comfortable. It's set up to first help you understand relationship problems and BPD and then guide you through common relationship challenges faced by people with BPD and their FP. The goal is to give you the knowledge and tools to tackle your relationship problems, helping you feel more connected, build stronger relationships, lessen your relationship problem areas, and grow beyond BPD. In working with individuals with BPD for over two decades, I can tell you it is possible to achieve your relationship goals. Never give up on yourself or in making the most out of your life. Let's dive in!

CHAPTER 1

Identifying Disruptive Factors in Relationships

Let's start by looking at the things in your relationship that might be causing problems, likely related to your borderline personality disorder (BPD). Relationships often deal with the same issues over and over, and how we see ourselves, others, and the world, including our FP, can be affected in both good and bad ways. BPD amplifies the complication of these issues and destructive tendencies but uncovering the underlying factors that add to the reasons they still exist will help empower you over your BPD. In this chapter, we're going to focus on you and creating the foundation for your relationship story.

The ten BPD relationship problem areas are common challenges that can disrupt your relationship with your FP, amplifying BPD urges, beliefs, behaviors, and patterns that increase the probability of relationship issues. For example, if you're often scared of being abandoned, you may become overbearing or needy, may always look for reassurance, or may even test the relationship to see if your FP truly cares. This may drive you to have unstable moods or pull away suddenly and give them the silent treatment, which can confuse and overwhelm your FP. Being very jealous or trying to control them might also push them away. These patterns can lead to frequent break-ups, mistrust, and difficulty believing in positive experiences, creating a cycle of emotional turmoil. By examining these problem areas and learning the skills you need, you can build a stronger bond with your FP, even while managing your BPD.

As you gain more emotional self-control, build recognition into your authentic self, and learn to communicate more openly about your emotions, desires, and needs, you can break these old maladaptive beliefs, behaviors, and patterns. Understanding how these problem areas impact your relationships can lead to healthier, more fulfilling connections, where both you and your FP feel more supported, heard, and understood.

Below are the top ten relationship problem areas, and if yours isn't on the list, that's okay. There's a spot for you to add your own if needed. As you go through this, think about your own experiences, specific triggers, behaviors, and patterns that might be instigating or amplifying these issues. The exercise after the list is going to help you further identify which ones cause the greatest relationship disruption. The goal isn't to blame anyone but to better understand what's going on beneath the surface.

The Ten BPD Relationship Problem Areas

1. Frequent fear of abandonment: You often think your FP is planning to leave you, even if there's no clear identifiable reason. This can make you hypervigilant and constantly seek reassurance or try to test how much your FP cares.

2. Overreaction to perceived slights: Small disagreements or feeling criticized make you react strongly. You might get very upset, pull away, or even do things that hurt yourself.

3. Unpredictable mood swings: You go from feeling very loving to very angry with your FP quickly, and sometimes it's unclear what caused it.

4. Excessive clinginess or neediness: Due to your fear of abandonment, you always check in, need a lot of attention and reassurance, or lean too much on your FP.

5. Sudden withdrawal or silent treatment: You easily feel hurt or misunderstood, so you suddenly stop talking or pull away.

6. Extreme jealousy and control issues: You feel extreme jealousy and try to control your FP by constantly wanting to know where they are, checking their phone, or controlling who they talk to.

7. Testing the relationship: You do things to see how much your FP cares, like flirting with other people, pushing them away to see if they'll come back, or starting unnecessary fights.

8. Frequent break-ups and make-ups: Your relationship has frequent separations, break-ups, and make-ups in a short time.

9. Difficulty in handling criticism: Feedback, small and intended to be helpful, tends to feel like a major personal attack, leading to overreactions, arguments, or feelings of worthlessness.

10. Difficulty trusting positive experiences: You struggle to believe that good things, like love or compliments, are genuine. You constantly doubt your FP's feelings, even when everything seems fine.

Your specific relationship problem area: _____

_____

These issues can create real challenges in relationships, often leading to misunderstandings, emotional exhaustion, and even trust problems. Managing them takes a lot of patience, understanding, and effort from both you and your FP. However, by learning specific skills and strategies, like how to handle emotional reactions, improve communication, and build trust, you can navigate these challenges more successfully and create a healthier, stronger connection.

Identifying Relationship Challenges

The exercise below will help you identify your top three BPD relationship problems. We'll be using this information as you go through the workbook to develop insight and build your personal growth and relationship strategies. For now, you'll be asked to rate how often each problem occurs and how much it affects your relationship with your FP. Rate each one from 0 (none at all) to 10 (happens every day and extreme negative impact).

1. Frequent fear of abandonment

    How often do you worry your FP will leave you, even without proof?

    0   1   2   3   4   5   6   7   8   9   10

    What's the degree of negative impact on your relationship?

    0   1   2   3   4   5   6   7   8   9   10

2. Overreaction to perceived slights

    How often do you overreact to small disagreements or criticisms?

    0   1   2   3   4   5   6   7   8   9   10

What's the degree of negative impact on your relationship?

0   1   2   3   4   5   6   7   8   9   10

3. Unpredictable mood swings

How often do your feelings for your FP swing from love to anger?

0   1   2   3   4   5   6   7   8   9   10

What's the degree of negative impact on your relationship?

0   1   2   3   4   5   6   7   8   9   10

4. Excessive clinginess or neediness

How often do you feel the need for constant attention or closeness with your FP?

0   1   2   3   4   5   6   7   8   9   10

What's the degree of negative impact on your relationship?

0   1   2   3   4   5   6   7   8   9   10

5. Sudden withdrawal or silent treatment

How often do you give your FP the silent treatment or suddenly withdraw when you feel hurt?

0   1   2   3   4   5   6   7   8   9   10

What's the degree of negative impact on your relationship?

0   1   2   3   4   5   6   7   8   9   10

6. Extreme jealousy and control issues

How often do you feel extremely jealous or try to control your FP's actions?

0   1   2   3   4   5   6   7   8   9   10

What's the degree of negative impact on your relationship?

0   1   2   3   4   5   6   7   8   9   10

7.   Testing the relationship

How often do you test your FP's love by creating conflicts or pushing them away?

0   1   2   3   4   5   6   7   8   9   10

What's the degree of negative impact on your relationship?

0   1   2   3   4   5   6   7   8   9   10

8.   Frequent break-ups and reconciliations

How often does your relationship go through separations, break-ups, and make-ups?

0   1   2   3   4   5   6   7   8   9   10

What's the degree of negative impact on your relationship?

0   1   2   3   4   5   6   7   8   9   10

9.   Difficulty handling criticism

How often do you intensely react to feedback that is small or intended to be helpful?

0   1   2   3   4   5   6   7   8   9   10

What's the degree of negative impact on your relationship?

0   1   2   3   4   5   6   7   8   9   10

10. Difficulty trusting positive experiences

How often do you doubt your FP's love or positive actions?

0   1   2   3   4   5   6   7   8   9   10

What's the degree of negative impact on your relationship?

0   1   2   3   4   5   6   7   8   9   10

11. Your specific relationship problem area:_____

How often does this occur?

0   1   2   3   4   5   6   7   8   9   10

What's the degree of negative impact on your relationship?

0   1   2   3   4   5   6   7   8   9   10

Find your top three BPD relationship problem areas based on your ratings and put them in the spaces below. If you have more than three, try your best to narrow it down to three. This might be hard, but for now, we want to focus on identifying the greatest and most impactful problems and building skills to manage them. Don't worry, you can always come back later and work on the other areas too.

1	2	3

Listing your top three BPD relationship problem areas and how often they occur and to what degree will help you notice not only when they arise but the intensity of them as well. The second part of this chapter is going to help you build insight into their origin and why they're still in your life. The next exercise may be hard for you. Allow yourself time to process the information and resist feeling pressured to get it all done in a hurry.

How They Started and Why They Stayed

The following exercise will help you build a deeper understanding of your top three relationship problem areas and why they've stayed around and attached to your BPD. These problem areas, like getting upset over small things, having mood swings, or not trusting when good things happen, are likely from past experiences and internalized beliefs, which helped create BPD behavior and patterns. When you think about relationship problems, you've likely noticed how they keep showing up, amplifying your feelings and driving you to react in ways that lead to arguments, hurt feelings, or misunderstandings. This causes you to easily feel stuck and hopeless when you keep repeating the same patterns again and again. It's time to be a pattern breaker, opening yourself up to new options and experiences that help you grow beyond your BPD.

By working through this exercise, you'll start to see how these beliefs and behaviors play a role in the creation and perpetuation of your BPD relationship problem areas. Let's tackle this!

How They Started

Start by reviewing the list of twenty possible reasons you developed BPD, such as emotional neglect or an unstable family environment. Check the boxes that match your experiences and then think about how each of these might have contributed to the creation of your top three relationship problem areas.

☐ **Emotional Invalidation**: When your feelings were often ignored or dismissed by others, especially as a child.

☐ **Physical Abuse**: Being physically hurt or punished in a way that was unfair or extreme.

☐ **Emotional Abuse**: Being mistreated emotionally by parents, caregivers, or others who were supposed to take care of you.

☐ **Neglect**: Not getting enough care, attention, or love when you needed it.

☐ **Unstable Family Life**: Growing up in a home with frequent arguments, break-ups, or fights.

☐ **Abandonment**: Feeling like important people in your life left you or didn't care about you.

☐ **Inconsistent Love**: Sometimes getting love and other times being ignored or punished without knowing why.

☐ **Harsh Criticism**: Constantly being criticized or judged harshly, making it hard to feel good about yourself.

☐ **Severe Punishment**: Receiving punishment that felt excessive or unjust.

☐ **Inconsistent Parenting**: Having parents who would change their behavior often, sometimes being very caring, and other times being distant or harsh.

☐ **Lack of Support**: Not having anyone to turn to when you needed help or advice.

☐ **Feeling Unloved**: Growing up feeling like you weren't loved or appreciated for who you are.

☐ **Witnessing Violence**: Seeing violence or abusive behavior in your home or environment.

☐ **Mental Health Issues in the Family**: Having family members with mental health issues that affected how they treated you.

☐ **Overprotective Parenting**: Having parents who were overly controlling, making you feel like you couldn't make decisions.

☐ **Chaotic Home Environment**: Living in a home that felt unpredictable, unsafe, or stressful most of the time.

☐ **Verbal Abuse**: Being yelled at, insulted, or threatened by those around you.

☐ **Parental Separation or Divorce**: Going through your parents separating or divorcing, causing confusion or fear about relationships.

☐ **Trauma**: Experiencing a traumatic event, like the loss of a loved one or witnessing something very scary or upsetting.

☐ **Bullying**: Being bullied or picked on by others, making you feel alone and insecure.

List any other possible origin that may not be listed above: _____

_____

Think about your top three relationship problem areas. For each one, write how your early life experiences might have shaped those problems. Use the space below each one to think about how things like mood swings, trust issues, or fear of being left may come from your past. If it feels like too much, it's okay to stop, take a break, or ask your therapist or FP to help you. This is about understanding where your struggles started and how they affect your relationships now. Be as honest as you can. You're doing this for you.

INSIGHT-GUIDING QUESTIONS:

1. Could your relationship problem area have started because you felt emotionally unsupported or invalidated in the past? For example, did people often ignore your feelings or make you feel like you couldn't express yourself?

2. Was there a time when you learned to expect people to leave you or stop caring about you? Did these feelings of abandonment continue into adult relationships, making it hard to trust others?

3. Think about whether your relationship problem areas are connected to experiences when you felt emotionally unsafe or criticized. Did you develop maladaptive beliefs, behaviors, and patterns because you were in environments that made you feel judged or inadequate?

Problem Area 1:_____

_____

_____

Problem Area 2:_____

_____

_____

Problem Area 3:_____

_____

_____

Why They Stayed

The next exercise is going to help you figure out why your BPD beliefs, behaviors, and patterns keep showing up in your relationships. Often, these behaviors were ways of protecting yourself from emotional pain or avoiding feelings of rejection or fear. But even though they may have helped in the past, they now cause harm to your relationships. To complete this exercise, think about how your current relationship problems may originate from past experiences, like emotional neglect or fear of abandonment. Then, look at the list of reasons why these behaviors continue, such as "to stay safe" or "to avoid abandonment," and describe, to the best of your ability, how they influence the perpetuation of your top three relationship issues.

Be as honest as you can. Understanding why these patterns started and what factors into them continuing can help you take the first step toward changing them and improving your relationships. There are also some insight-encouraging questions to help you after the list.

☐ **To Stay Safe**: Engaging in certain behaviors, even hurtful ones, helps you feel protected from emotional pain.

☐ **To Avoid Facing Fears**: Avoiding challenges or changes keeps you from dealing with the fear of failure or loss.

☐ **To Avoid Abandonment**: You use controlling or manipulative behaviors to prevent people from leaving.

☐ **To Feel in Control**: Acting out helps you feel in control when your emotions are overwhelming.

☐ **To Validate Negative Self-View**: You behave in ways that confirm your belief that you're unlovable or worthless.

☐ **Fear of Being Vulnerable**: Keeping emotional walls up protects you from being hurt, even if it damages relationships.

☐ **To Get Attention**: Extreme behaviors may be used to get attention or care from others, even if it's negative attention.

☐ **To Avoid Rejection**: By pushing others away first, you avoid the possibility of being rejected.

☐ **Emotional Numbing**: Engaging in risky or self-harming behaviors blocks out painful emotions.

☐ **To Avoid Disappointment**: You expect the worst in relationships, so you sabotage things to avoid feeling let down.

☐ **To Feel Emotionally Protected**: You hold onto defensive behaviors to shield yourself from feeling emotionally exposed.

☐ **To Feel Important**: Dramatic actions make you feel like you matter, even when the result is negative.

☐ **To Gain Power**: You use manipulative behaviors to feel more powerful in relationships.

☐ **To Validate Emotional Instability**: Your chaotic behaviors match how unstable you feel inside, reinforcing your beliefs.

☐ **To Avoid Feeling Inadequate**: You engage in behaviors that make others feel guilty, avoiding feelings of not being enough.

☐ **To Test Loyalty**: Pushing people away helps you see if others will come back, proving loyalty.

☐ **To Control Anxiety**: Repeating the same behaviors helps you manage the anxiety you feel when things change.

☐ **To Confirm Fears About Relationships**: You behave in ways that confirm your belief that all relationships are unstable.

☐ **To Feel Less Alone**: Negative behaviors may be a way to make sure others stay involved with you, even if it's through conflict.

☐ **To Avoid Emotional Growth**: Sticking to old patterns keeps you from facing the hard work of emotional growth and change.

INSIGHT-GUIDING QUESTIONS:

1. What behaviors do you continue to engage in because they make you feel safe, even if they harm your relationships? For example, you might avoid addressing problems in the relationship to stay emotionally protected, but this can prevent genuine and open connection and allow issues to build up over time.

2. How might the beliefs you developed about yourself, like thinking you're unlovable or always going to be abandoned, still affect how you interact in relationships today? For example, do you push people away before they can leave you?

3. What emotions are you trying to avoid when you repeat certain behaviors, such as emotional numbing or acting out? For instance, are you avoiding feelings of rejection or fear of failure?

Problem Area 1:_____

_____

_____

Problem Area 2:_____

_____

_____

Problem Area 3:_____

_____

_____

Great job! I know this was not an easy task. Insight building can be a scary thing, but it's a necessary process to help you have stronger relationships with everyone you know, including your FP. You may want to return to this chapter from time to time and redo it as you learn more skills and start to see changes in yourself and in your relationships.

The information in this chapter will guide you as you progress through the workbook. It will help you expand your thinking and understand that there are different ways to manage BPD beliefs, behaviors, and patterns. You'll see that there are options and possibilities for positive changes, allowing you to embrace the love and caring that you, and everyone, deserve in life.

Setting the Stage for Relationship Success

Using the spaces below, pull together what you learned from this chapter so you can take this information with you and use it in your relationships.

How will what you've learned in this chapter help you manage your top three BPD relationship problem areas?

_____

_____

_____

In what ways can this knowledge help you respond more calmly to disagreements or feedback?

_____

_____

_____

What can you take from this chapter that can help you have greater mood stabilization and consistency in your relationship?

_____

_____

_____

What can you use from this chapter to build a closer relationship with your FP?

_____

_____

_____

How can what you've learned in this chapter help you increase trust, acceptance, and love in your relationship?

_____

_____

_____

In the next chapter, we're going to dive deeper into understanding BPD and how to explain it to your FP. You'll start with a BPD FAQ and explore the BPD paradox, how some protective behaviors harm your relationships, and what strengthens or weakens your connections. Self-determination and empowered choice is what lies ahead, so let's not wait, let's get to it!

CHAPTER 2

Understanding BPD and Explaining It to Your Favorite Person

Talking to your FP about borderline personality disorder isn't easy and can be very confusing, overwhelming, and frightening for everyone involved. BPD is one of the most confusing mental health conditions, both for those living with it and for those treating it. But confusing doesn't mean it's impossible or hopeless to manage. BPD can be treated, and you can learn strategies to manage the thoughts, behaviors, and patterns that disrupt your relationships and life. It's important to realize and internalize this. If you don't believe in yourself, it's harder for your FP to believe in you too. Building faith in yourself is difficult, especially since BPD tends to distort how you see yourself, others, and your world, but it's a crucial first step. Let's take a look at Sarah and how she deals with BPD and its effects on her relationships.

• Sarah, Her Symptoms, and Her Relationships

Sarah is 28 and works at a marketing agency. She tries hard to succeed but often feels trapped in emotional chaos because of her BPD. She's identified her top three relationship problem areas as frequent fear of abandonment, extreme jealousy and control issues, and trouble trusting positive experiences.

One of Sarah's biggest challenges is her frequent fear of abandonment as she constantly worries that her FP, Chris, will suddenly leave her. This makes her frequently seek reassurance, keeping her on high alert for any and all signs of abandonment. Her anxiety over Chris tends to spill into her work, making it hard for her to focus if she's worried about what he's doing or whether he's about to end their relationship. But she has difficulty pinpointing a clear reason for this fear, only that she "feels it's coming."

Sarah's extreme jealousy and control issues affect both her work and her relationship with Chris. She gets anxious if she doesn't know where Chris is at all times and sometimes checks his phone and tries to control who he talks to because she fears he'll find someone else. Doing this often leads to arguments, adding more stress to her life and creating tension between them.

Sarah also has difficulty accepting feedback, which she tends to interpret as criticism. Even when it's positive, she feels like it's an attack on her abilities, leaving her feeling inadequate and broken. She also finds it hard to trust positive experiences, feeling unsure whether they're genuine, which makes her feel vulnerable and defenseless. One time at work, her boss complimented a project she completed, saying, "You did a great job, but adding more data could make it even better." Although it was a genuine compliment, and Sarah and her boss always got along, Sarah only focused on the part suggesting improvement and instantly felt like a failure. This led to feelings of worthlessness. Later, when Chris praised her for the same project, she couldn't accept it, thinking he was lying and talking down to her, so she started yelling at him and calling him a liar. This continual doubting of feedback and praise feeds her insecurity and leaves her stuck in a cycle of self-doubt, which fuels her BPD and relationship issues.

Sarah's relationships have historically been chaotic. When she feels hurt, Sarah pushes people away, but at the same time, she clings to them for validation, overwhelming her friends and past and present FPs, including Chris. When they seem frustrated with her, she feels rejected and either lashes out or shuts down entirely. Despite encouragement from her family and Chris to seek help, Sarah feared being judged and wouldn't go, but after a breakdown at work, her boss referred her to a mental health program. At first, she went just to avoid losing her job, but she soon realized that getting help was the first step toward building self-control and managing her issues.

In therapy, Sarah learned to identify her BPD relationship problem areas and manage her BPD symptoms. She began to understand that her fears and jealousy were part of her condition and not a reflection of reality. Using strategies from therapy, she started to improve her relationships. Over time, Sarah discovered that a life without constant chaos was possible. With effort, she began to experience longer periods of stability and well-being. Sarah's journey shows how tough BPD can make relationships, but with tools and support, she found hope and strength to move forward in her recovery and build healthier relationships.

Sarah faced her BPD and relationship issues head-on. She worked hard to challenge her thoughts, actions, and habits so she could have a better relationship. You can do this too. The skills you'll gain from this workbook are designed to help you build the kinds of relationships you really want. Is it easy? No, but it's definitely possible. It all starts with understanding BPD better. Once you know more, you'll be able to explain it to your FP in a way that makes sense and helps them understand more about what you're going through.

Let's dive in by reviewing the answers to some frequently asked questions about BPD and begin your journey toward healthier relationships!

The BPD FAQ and Answers

Over the last twenty years, I've worked with many people with BPD, and these are some common questions and answers I've been asked. I've kept the answers short, so you won't feel overwhelmed. If you feel comfortable, share these with your FP, so you both can have a clear understanding as you start this process.

What is Borderline Personality Disorder (BPD)?

BPD is a mental health condition in which people experience intense mood swings, impulsive actions, and unstable relationships. People with BPD often have trouble controlling their emotions, leading to strong emotional reactions and impulsive behaviors, like reckless spending, acting out, self-hatred, or using substances. They might also feel empty inside and be scared of being abandoned, making it hard for them to feel like they belong. This can cause rocky relationships where they may really like someone one moment and then push them away the next. Some people with BPD also hurt themselves as a way to deal with intense emotions, stress, or fear, or to feel in control. Even though BPD is tough, with the right therapy and support, people with BPD can learn to manage their symptoms and live meaningful lives.

How do you know if someone has BPD?

Identifying BPD involves noticing prolonged patterns like intense emotional ups and downs, impulsive actions, and unstable relationships. People often make mistakes by overestimating a few behaviors while missing others, which leads to confusion about the disorder. That's why it's important to get an official diagnosis from a qualified mental health professional who can accurately identify BPD.

What causes BPD?

We're not looking to blame anyone when trying to understand BPD causes. Instead, it's about learning why BPD might develop so you can take control of it. The exact cause isn't fully known, but research shows that BPD usually develops from a mix of genetics, biology, and life experiences. For example, if someone in your family has a mental health disorder, you might be at higher risk for BPD.

Also, experiencing childhood abuse, neglect, or growing up in an unstable home can increase the chances of developing BPD, as these experiences can make it hard to manage emotions, behaviors, and relationships. But not everyone with these experiences will develop BPD, which means other personal factors, like genetics and various life events, also play a role.

Can BPD be cured?

The word "cure" means to completely get rid of a disease or condition, but that doesn't apply to personality disorders like BPD, or other mental health and medical conditions. There isn't a cure for BPD, but that doesn't mean it can't be managed. With the right strategies and coping skills, you can learn to control BPD, so it doesn't control your life. Think of it like a chronic illness, it may not go away completely, but treatment can help reduce symptoms and improve your overall well-being.

Do you need medication for BPD?

Medication can help with things like depression, anxiety, or impulse control issues that often accompany BPD, but there's no medicine that removes core BPD issues like fear of abandonment or feelings of emptiness. Sometimes, people expect medication to solve these issues, leading to higher doses and side effects. While medication can be helpful in managing moods and some thinking distortions, learning skills and strategies is the key to managing the issues and reactions patterns associated with BPD and reducing its negative impact on your life.

Can someone with BPD have "normal" relationships?

Yes, they can! With insight, learning management strategies, and practice, people with BPD can improve how they communicate, handle their emotions, and control their actions during tough times. Over time, with patience and support, people with BPD can have stable and fulfilling relationships.

Is BPD the same as bipolar disorder?

No, BPD and bipolar disorder are not the same, but some people have both. They can seem similar because some symptoms overlap. Bipolar disorder causes mood swings that last weeks or months—highs (mania or hypomania) and lows (depression). BPD causes fast mood changes, sometimes in minutes or hours. For example, someone with BPD might get very angry, act out, and then quickly feel calm and want closeness again.

Mood changes in bipolar disorder often happen without a clear reason. In BPD, mood shifts usually happen after something upsetting happens. People with bipolar disorder often feel okay between episodes. People with BPD often struggle more with steady moods and relationships unless they get good treatment.

What should my FP know about BPD?

It's important to be honest and clear with your FP (favorite person) about BPD. Let them know that change takes time, and you're learning to see yourself, others, and the world in a more balanced way, with less fear and conflict. BPD isn't about choosing to act out; it's more like reacting as if you're stuck or in danger, even when you're not. Be open about what you're working on and what you're afraid of. Let your FP support you so you can face harmful thoughts and behaviors together. This workbook and online tools for your FP can help you both grow closer while you get the support you need to heal.

Now that you've read these FAQs, take a moment to think about how your FP might take in this info. Just like you're learning new ways to cope, they'll need time to learn how to help you, themselves, and the relationship. Knowing these common questions can help you prepare to talk with your FP and ask for their help. BPD isn't always obvious. Sometimes it shows up in quiet, confusing ways. This adds to the mixed-up, back-and-forth nature of BPD—something we'll talk more about next.

The BPD Paradox

BPD is a tricky opponent. It doesn't work in a straightforward way, but in a confusing and contradictory manner. It gets you to do things that work against your own needs, making it harder for you to see yourself, others, and your relationships clearly. This is what we call the BPD paradox, and it can really mess with how you view the world. A paradox is something that contradicts itself, like giving a thumbs up when you actually mean something is bad. That would leave you confused, because a thumbs up usually means something good, but here it's saying the opposite. It's pretty confusing, right? Let's take a look at how the BPD paradox rears its ugly head in Sarah and Chris's relationship.

Sarah's life with Chris is often confusing because of the BPD paradox. Her biggest fear is that Chris will leave her, and this fear drives her to act in ways that push him away, even though all she wants is reassurance. For example, Sarah's fear of abandonment makes her overly suspicious of Chris. She starts watching his every move, looking for signs that he might be planning to leave. Chris senses her tension and becomes visibly anxious, which only makes Sarah's anxiety worse. Her BPD starts telling her, "He's hiding something! He's going to leave you!" This leads her to aggressively confront Chris, demanding answers.

Chris, confused, tells her, "I'm not doing anything like that. That's crazy!" But her BPD twists his words, making her feel like he's calling her crazy and lying to her. She becomes more agitated, and the argument escalates until Chris storms out. Her BPD then tells her, "See, I was right! He left you," even though her fear-driven behavior is what caused the argument.

Sarah's BPD paradox tricks her into creating the very abandonment she fears, making it hard for her to feel secure. But through building insight and skills, she's learning to recognize this pattern and take steps toward healthier, more stable relationships.

The BPD paradox plays out in a variety of different ways, not just with fear of abandonment. It has many tools at its disposal, like splitting (seeing things as all good or all bad), distorting your view of self, others, and your world, and causing you to see calm and neutral moments as threatening. These BPD tools often lead to paradoxical situations where your perceptions shift dramatically, often without a clear, rational basis, resulting in inconsistencies and conflicts in your interactions and self-perception.

The way to resolve the paradox is to make the heart of the matter self-evident and identify evidence to its contrary. This means we have to make it obvious, not let it work behind the scenes amplifying your BPD relationship problem areas, and instead help you embrace not only your BPD fears but confront them by empowering yourself.

Let's revisit Sarah's fear of abandonment as illustrated above, but this time let's make the heart of the matter self-evident so you can see the difference.

Sarah was feeling really anxious and afraid that Chris, her FP, might leave her. This fear made her question his true motives and intentions for their relationship. Deep down, she knew it was her fear of abandonment, a part of her BPD, trying to take control. Feeling overwhelmed, Sarah walked up to Chris and said, "I'm getting nervous and uneasy that you don't want to be with me, that you're going to abandon me." Chris, knowing about her BPD struggles, calmly replied, "I hear what you're saying, but let's figure out what triggered this fear." Sarah thought for a moment and said, "I was scrolling through social media and saw a post about some girl's boyfriend suddenly leaving her. I'm worried that could happen to me too." Chris gently reminded her, "I understand your fear, but we need to focus on what's happening in our relationship, not someone else's." By sharing her feelings openly with Chris, and disclosing the heart of the matter, Sarah recognized her fear of abandonment and communicated it, allowing Chris to support her in a way that helped her feel more secure.

As you read this scenario, you probably noticed it's much more controlled and calm. Sarah asserted herself and made her fear and the evidence against it self-evident, significantly decreasing the impact of the BPD paradox. This decreased the likelihood of maladaptive behaviors induced by fear of abandonment.

Now that you've learned about the BPD paradox, let's build your skills to change it. By doing this, you can significantly lessen the likelihood of the first Sarah and Chris scenario and move toward the second.

From Paradox to Self-Evident

Four of the most likely BPD heart-of-the-matter areas that amplify your paradox are listed. This is not an all-inclusive list, so there's an extra blank for you to add your specific issue if it's not listed.

In the blanks below, describe your BPD paradox within the domains listed. If you feel you don't have a BPD paradox related to one or more of the domains, that's fine, just complete the ones you do. For the paradox blank, describe what behavior you engage in that increases the probability of you ending up with exactly what you were afraid of in the first place. For the heart-of-the-matter issue, make it self-evident. Clearly describe how you can cut through the confusion by being assertive with your FP, just like in the second scenario. I know this can be confusing, so I added some insight-building questions and provided examples from Sarah's situation to help you.

1. What specific event or action triggered your BPD fears, doubts, and other intense emotions and thoughts?

2. How did your reaction affect the situation, and was it helpful or hurtful?

3. Is there clear evidence to support your feelings, or could they be influenced by past experiences or assumptions?

4. What could you directly communicate to express your feelings, so others clearly understand and respond in a helpful way?

Fear of abandonment paradox: When I feel scared that Chris might leave me, I start acting in ways that push him away. I get upset easily, ask him a lot of questions to see if he really cares about me, and sometimes I even ignore him because I'm so worried he'll leave. When I do this, it makes him feel stressed or like he's always having to prove he cares. Then, he needs space, and that makes me feel like he's actually leaving me, which is what I was scared of all along.

Fear of abandonment self-evident: I know my fear of Chris leaving comes from inside me because it happens even when he's being nice and caring. It's not about what he's doing, it's about how I feel and my thoughts. I get triggered by small things, like seeing other people's relationship problems or if Chris is busy, and I start to believe that he'll leave me too.

Fear of abandonment paradox: Describe how your fear of abandonment leads you to engage in behaviors that push your FP away, leading you to feel abandoned by the person you feared would abandon you.

_____

_____

_____

_____

Fear of abandonment self-evident: Clearly state the BPD fears, doubts, and other intense emotions and thoughts in simple, clear language and discuss it using compelling, concrete evidence.

_____

_____

_____

_____

Self-worth paradox: What behaviors do you tend to engage in that enhance the feelings of low self-worth as opposed to feeling empowered?

_____

_____

_____

_____

Self-worth self-evident: Clearly explain BPD fears, doubts, and emotions using simple language and strong evidence.

_____

_____

_____

_____

Rejection sensitivity paradox: What behaviors do you tend to engage in that increase the likelihood you will be or feel rejected, such as talking over others, not listening, being unable to express yourself clearly, or violating others' boundaries, instead of gaining a sense of acceptance?

_____

_____

_____

_____

Rejection sensitivity self-evident: Clearly explain BPD fears, doubts, and emotions using simple language and strong evidence.

_____

_____

_____

_____

Emptiness paradox: What behaviors do you tend to engage in that increase the likelihood you will enhance your feeling of emptiness, such as isolating yourself instead of confronting your fears, or deriding yourself as opposed to engaging in self-reflection about what activated this feeling?

_____

_____

_____

_____

Emptiness self-evident: Clearly explain BPD fears, doubts, and emotions using simple language and strong evidence.

_____

_____

_____

_____

Now that you've uncovered your BPD paradox and have started building your skills by making your heart-of-the-matter issues self-evident, you're ready to examine the factors that erode and enhance your BPD relationship problem areas. Building strong relationships beyond BPD is a cumulative process, like building a Lego® tower, one brick on top of the other, while supporting the entire structure.

What Empowers and Detracts from Your Relationships

Next, we'll look at the top ten relationship factors for people with BPD, five that empower you and five that hurt you. These factors usually don't show up one by one. Instead, they tend to rush in all at once, overwhelming you and pushing you back into old, unhealthy patterns that damage your self-worth and relationships. To handle this "horde," we need to break it into smaller, manageable pieces. This helps you figure out which factors have the biggest or smallest effect on you and your relationships.

As you go through this exercise, try to make it personal. Think about your own values, views, and behaviors. That way, when your "horde" shows up, you can spot it and step aside before BPD reactions take over. This helps you avoid feeding the negative and instead focus on what empowers you and strengthens your relationships.

Learning and using this skill will help you enhance self-control so you can determine how you, and not your BPD, are going to respond, while also helping you communicate clearly with your FP about BPD issues while they join you on this journey.

My Relationship Detracting and Empowering Factors

The five detractors are listed first in the columns below, followed by the five empowering factors. In the left column are the titles and descriptions. The right column is for you to describe how each of these factors show up in your life and relationships and their impact. After you've completed your description of how these show up in your life, rank them in order from most to least impactful using the chart below.

The full description may describe your experience fully or partly. That's ok. If partly, then write how it partly shows up in your life and relationships. The important part is that you realize and recognize how these factors manifest so you can enhance the empowering ones and minimize the detracting ones.

	Relationship Detracting Factor	How It Manifests for You
1	**Invalidation**: Responses that dismiss your thoughts, feelings, emotions, or behaviors as invalid or unimportant can make you feel misunderstood, rejected, or overwhelmed. This can cause you to react in a heightened, distressing, and emotionally dysregulated manner.	

	Relationship Detracting Factor	How It Manifests for You
2	**Fearing Abandonment**: An intensive emotional and psychological experience that someone is going to give up on you completely, leading you psychologically destitute. This can cause you to over-attach to someone, demand they do something to make you feel safe, or inadvertently push them away.	
3	**Codependency**: This is an over-dependency on someone that reinforces maladaptive patterns that prevent personal growth and self-efficacy due to an overreliance on someone for your sense of self-worth or identity. This can cause feelings of inadequacy and dependency by taking away your personal power.	
4	**Conflict and Instability**: Relationships marked by frequent disputes, volatility, or unpredictability caused by differences in opinion, beliefs, experiences, or personality. This can decrease the ability to regulate your emotions and maintain a sense of safety. High-conflict relationships can exacerbate symptoms and contribute to emotional dysregulation.	
5	**Enabling Behaviors**: These are actions that enable or excuse someone else's problematic behaviors, including those they should be taking responsibility for and managing themselves. This can indirectly reinforce unhealthy and destructive patterns and hinder personal growth.	

	Relationship Detracting Factor	How It Manifests for You
1	**Emotional Support**: The act of showing understanding, compassion, and love that helps you manage intense emotions, rejection sensitivity, and feelings of emptiness. This can help you feel more secure and less alone through nonjudgmental active listening and validation of your experience.	
2	**Consistency**: Predictable patterns and actions that enable building a sense of confidence, stability, and security in your connections. Knowing that you have someone you can rely on during times of distress can help lessen anxiety and the risk of self- and relationship-destructive behaviors.	
3	**Acceptance**: The willingness to love and value a partner as they are, including their flaws. This can help you feel supported when trying to manage your feelings and experiences, and it can even reduce those feelings of invalidation and self-doubt.	
4	**Healthy Models**: Internalized or learned beliefs and understanding of trust, respect, safety, acceptance, freedom of choice, positive communication, conflict management, and fun. These can provide you with tools to recognize and incorporate healthy communication, boundaries, and conflict resolution skills into your relationships.	

	Relationship Detracting Factor	How It Manifests for You
5	**Attachment-Based Relationships**: You're each other's safe haven and secure base and have a level of commitment and understanding that helps you feel safe and heard. These can be relationships with a therapist or an FP, as they help you develop coping skills, improve emotion regulation, and build healthier relationships.	

Using the chart below, rank the different factors on how impactful they are to you and your relationships: 1=Not at all impactful, 3=Neutral, 5=Most impactful. You may be thinking, *what if all of the detractors are 5?* Then they're all 5 and that's ok, because now you know to be on the lookout for all of them. The goal is to help you be more aware and catch them. You do this by knowing how they manifest, making them easier to spot. No more hiding in the darkness of overwhelm and capitulation.

	Detracting Factors		Empowering Factors
	Invalidation		Emotional Support
	Fearing Abandonment		Consistency
	Codependency		Acceptance
	Conflict and Instability		Healthy Models
	Enabling Behaviors		Attachment-Based Relationships

You've taken an important step by gaining insight into your relationships. That's a big deal. BPD can be sneaky, and after exercises like this, it often fights back. You might hear thoughts like, *You'll never have a good relationship* or *You don't deserve love*. That's actually a sign you're making progress. Keep going.

Yes, it's scary, but you *can* do this. BPD often tries to isolate you from support. But now, you've learned more about how BPD works and how it affects your relationships. You've also started building new skills to see yourself, others, and your world more clearly.

It's okay to feel afraid. Just don't stop. You're learning how to move past old patterns and open yourself to the life and love you want. These skills will help you feel more stable, more connected, and more empowered. Keep going, you're on your way.

Setting the Stage for Relationship Success

Using the spaces below, pull together what you learned from this chapter so you can take this information with you and use it in your relationships.

How will the skills you've learned in this chapter help you manage your top three BPD relationship problem areas?

_____

_____

_____

_____

In what ways can the skills you've learned in this chapter help you respond more calmly to disagreements or feedback?

_____

_____

_____

_____

What skills can you apply from this chapter to have greater mood stabilization and maintain consistency in your relationship?

_____

_____

_____

What can you use from this chapter to build a close relationship with your FP?

_____

_____

_____

_____

How can the skills you've learned in this chapter help you increase trust, acceptance, and love in your relationship?

_____

_____

_____

_____

Gaining a better understanding of BPD and how to explain it to your FP is a powerful first step. The next chapter will focus on understanding what makes a good relationship so you can spot the good and avoid the bad.

CHAPTER 3

BPD Relationships 101

Many of your relationships have been disrupted by your BPD and its influence over you. BPD often creates a "distortion barrier" that blocks you from learning the basics of healthy relationships. Relationships are full of mystery, which can stir up fear, regret, doubt, or shame. But they can also bring hope, comfort, excitement, and peace, especially when they're healthy. The problem is, BPD often clings to fear more than the good stuff, partly because you may not have learned the basic building blocks of healthy relationships yet.

That's not your fault, it's just something you haven't learned yet. This chapter will teach you what you need to know. You might be surprised to see how BPD has twisted your view, and how different your life and relationships can feel once you begin to see things more clearly.

These concepts and processes can be very confusing, so we're going to get some help from Barbara and William and take a look at how BPD blocks their healthy relationship growth. You're also going to learn the skills to decrease the thoughts that have kept you stuck in maladaptive beliefs, behaviors, and patterns.

• Barbara and William

Barbara and William met on a website for people seeking long-term relationships. William had been divorced for three years and Barbara never married. Her longest relationship was six months. They would text and videochat every day. William felt an instant "click," and Barbara felt the same, as they would often joke and tease each other about it. As their mutual interest grew, they wanted to meet in real life. Barbara suggested meeting at a small bistro near where she lived at the end of the week, and William agreed.

A few days passed and they were about to meet. Barbara was excited, but she started remembering all those "truths" about men her mother and sisters told her. Men don't listen, they lie, are all users, and only want one thing. This old familiar voice echoed through her, and she embraced it as she always did. Acting on instinct, she texted William accusing him of only wanting her for sex and how he would eventually leave her lonely and broken. William responded, perplexed as to where she got this idea and asking, "What did I do?"

BPD was in control and Barbara began furiously texting William all the thoughts, memories, and feelings she had learned and experienced in her past. She wrote, "Of course you'd say that! You want me to be another stupid girl you trick into sleeping with you so you can use me up and throw me away. You only agreed to meet me to stand me up, leave me wondering, wanting, and waiting, and ultimately, I'll be all alone. You only wanted me as another notch on your bedpost of women you've hurt." William read the texts and then he received a video message. His head reeling with confusion, he opened it. Barbara was crouched down in the corner of her room sobbing and saying, "See what you did, you lying bastard!"

William deleted the messages, blocked Barbara and wondered what happened to bring this about. Barbara's BPD took control, and she followed its guidance, solidifying its presence inside her, causing it to feel vindicated. Right after she was excited about meeting him and felt the hope of starting a relationship with someone she liked, the BPD appeared like an evil genie out of a bottle next to her and insisted, "See, I was right. He was a user like mom and your sisters told you. I'm always right and I'll protect you. The hurt you feel only makes me right."

The story of William and Barbara may be one you can relate to as a whole or only in part. When you read through the story you can see that with the "right amount of distance" Barbara felt safe, but as soon as she took steps to be closer to someone and felt hope, those old beliefs, behaviors, and patterns were ignited, driving her to engage and fulfill that maladaptive, self-fulling prophecy that "everyone hurts you and everyone leaves." This doesn't have to be you. You can manage your relationship fears and perspectives differently. In this story, Barbara lacks the self-understanding and adaptive understanding of relationships, which would have helped her work through her fears, keep her BPD at bay, and continue her relationship with William.

You don't have to be Barbara. Let's get started doing it differently, by actively building a strong foundation of knowledge about relationships that will empower you to approach them with new perspectives and tools.

What Makes a Good Relationship?

The five components that make up a good relationship include open communication, listening and feeling heard, talking openly about emotions and physical desires, trusting yourself and the other person, and working through disagreements. These are some tall orders, so let's break them down into useful, practical parts to build those foundational skills that will help you manage your BPD relationship problem areas.

Open Communication

Open communication is more than just saying what's on your mind. It's speaking in a way that encourages empathy and compassion. This approach may be very frightening and overwhelming, but that's your BPD talking you into those maladaptive beliefs, behaviors, and patterns just like it did for Barbara. For the exercise below, you're going to identify what open communication skills you already have, and then you'll mark what communication skills you want to have. It's ok for these to be different, as this is part of the growth and skill-building process.

IDENTIFYING YOUR OPEN COMMUNICATION SKILLS

Go through the list and mark which skills you feel you have and use to communicate with your FP regularly in the "Have" column. If you don't have that particular skill but you wish you did or want to, put a mark in the "Want" column. Remember, no one is keeping score, so don't be overly critical and force yourself to mark skills you feel are not fully developed or those you rarely use.

Have	Want	Communication Skills
		Check your feelings—you take time to pause and reflect on how your body and mind are feeling (are you tense with clenched fists, thoughts becoming foggy and unclear?)
		Be empathetic—you understand the feelings of the other person and share your own clearly.
		Establish boundaries—you know what boundaries are important to you in various areas of your life (e.g., personal space, time, emotions, values).
		Find compromise—you're able to find common ground that addresses both your needs and concerns.
		Be respectful—you're able to avoid interrupting, fully attend to the speaker, and show respect for the other person's boundaries.
		Ask questions—you're clear and concise, encourage detailed and thoughtful responses, and adapt your language and tone to the situation.
		Respond rather than react—you pause, breathe, reflect on your emotions, choose your words carefully, focus on solutions, and seek understanding.

Have	Want	Communication Skills
		Keep checking in—you plan specific times for check-ins, whether they're daily, weekly, or monthly to see how you and your FP are doing (when relationship is calm, not only when in upheaval).
		Not hiding your feelings—you're able to embrace your emotions without judgment and express your feelings in a manner that feels comfortable for you and that encourages your FP to share their feelings.
		Think about timing—You choose the right moment to share your message, prioritizing urgency when needed and waiting for a better time for less critical topics.
		Avoid criticism—you're able to stay calm, focus on the topic at hand, not get triggered, seek understanding and empathize. You're able to express gratitude, not react defensively, use a growth mindset, and provide support for your FP.
		Supportive feedback—You communicate clearly by highlighting positives, addressing negatives without personalizing, encouraging improvement, listening sincerely, offering suggestions, and ensuring your non-verbal cues align with supportive words.
		Speak gently—you're able to speak in a calm, steady, and slow tone, using polite language while actively listening, and allow your FP to speak without interruption.
		Stay focused—You actively listen by understanding the message, minimizing distractions (e.g., phone off), and showing engagement through eye contact, nodding, and verbal cues.
		Be honest—You communicate clearly and directly, address the situation without blame, and show openness to your FP's perspective.

Now you know which open communication skills you already have and which ones you want. For the next step, write out your top three skills from the "Have" or "Want" column that serve you best, or can help you the most. Then, write down how you can incorporate them into your communication style to communicate openly with your FP in an adaptive and healthy way.

Top Three Open Communication Skills
1.
2.
3.

Although you focused on your top three, don't stop learning and including the other communication skills; but add them slowly. You want to build skills and not rush to pack them all in, which will cause you to feel overwhelmed and want to stop trying altogether.

Use these open communication skills to feel closer and more genuine with your FP and encourage growth beyond your BPD. The next step to making a good relationship is harnessing and building your ability to listen while feeling heard.

Listening and Feeling Heard

Your BPD tells you that the only way to be heard is by being loud, aggressive, or demanding. But this actually pushes people away, which is the opposite of what you want. This is part of the BPD paradox (see chapter 1). BPD makes you believe that if someone gives in, it means they love you and you're safe. But real safety and connection come from building a strong foundation over time. BPD tends to erode those foundational blocks, making things unstable.

Feeling heard makes you feel present, accepted, and safe, and it helps your FP feel that way too. BPD tells you that feeling safe won't last or will just lead to more pain. That belief has hurt you long enough. Let's look at the thoughts, feelings, and actions that help you and your FP feel truly heard. These are tools you *can* use, starting now.

WHEN I FEEL LISTENED TO AND HEARD

Below are several sentence stems for you to complete to help you explore what you or someone else can do to feel listened to and heard. Reflect on and express your experiences of being listened to and heard to provide insights into what makes communication meaningful and supportive for you. Your BPD is going to convince you otherwise, but stay the course and focus your listening energy on feeling heard and all that it entails. Answer as many of the stems as you can and catch those negatives and critiques that may creep into your mind. This exercise is for you and your FP—your BPD isn't invited.

When I share my thoughts, I feel listened to and heard when _____

_____

_____

I feel truly heard when someone (identify behaviors) _____

_____

_____

I know I'm being heard when someone (what evidence can you identify) _____

_____

_____

I feel most understood when someone _____

_____

_____

I appreciate it when someone shows they're listening by (identify behaviors) _____

_____

_____

When I express my emotions, feeling heard looks like _____

_____

_____

In a supportive conversation, I notice I am heard when someone _____

_____

_____

When someone validates my experiences, I feel _____

_____

_____

_____

I value it when someone takes the time to ask me _____

_____

_____

_____

Feeling listened to and heard is the result of getting your emotional needs met and responded to in a clear manner from both you and the person you're interacting with, whether your FP, or someone else. These needs can be safety, patience, autonomy, empathy, intimacy, acceptance, and so on. Look over your responses—do you see any needs, explicit or implicit, being conveyed? If so, write them in the My Heard Box below. If not, don't be discouraged. Include the emotional need you want to be conveyed that helps you feel listened to and heard.

My Heard Box

Use this knowledge to increase your insight into conversational and relationship strengtheners. What you don't want to do is use these responses as a "test" to see if your FP cares about you. That's BPD trickery. Testing degrades relationships because typically the person giving the test doesn't let the other know that they're going to be judged, so they fail, which empowers your BPD.

Last, ask yourself how you can use your responses and insight to not only help yourself feel heard but how you can show your FP that they're listened to and heard. What's their need? This can be a great experience, and any relationship worth your time and energy deserves it.

Trusting Yourself and Others

Trusting yourself and others is at the center of all relationships, and we're dealing with this after communication and listening because it's built upon these critical bedrock components. It's not easy to trust yourself when your BPD is tearing at your sense of self and making you question your value. When your value of self is tenuous, so is your sense of self-trust. This causes you to question your decisions, leading you to externalize your worth and validation. When this happens, you're always on the lookout for what you're not getting and how and if someone responds to what you say and do the "right" way. This is part of your BPD's deceit of your true self. But it's time to challenge these beliefs and build behaviors and patterns that move you forward, beyond your BPD. First, let's examine how much you trust yourself.

TRUSTING YOURSELF

You build trust in yourself by engaging in behaviors that increase the probability of a positive outcome. Your BPD tells you that if the world is not exactly as you expect it to be, then it's against you. It drove you to believe that if you're not getting the guarantee of the perfect expected outcome, don't do it, don't try it, and just accept that you're lost and meant to suffer all alone forever.

These are old BPD tactics that have been used long enough to siphon away your self-trust. Building self-trust entails practicing and enhancing your self-awareness, challenging your negative self-talk, taking action to build confidence, and nurturing who you are and those valuable parts of yourself. The exercise below is going to help you embark on this journey, and then we're going to further empower you by using this as a springboard to trust others.

BUILDING MY TRUSTED SELF

Review the strategies for building self-trust listed below in the left column. Think about what you can do, what actions you can take to put these strategies to work for you, then write them down in the right column. A guided journal for self-growth and understanding can be a great tool to reflect on your positive self. Also, if you find it too challenging to identify actions to put your strategies to work, try asking a mental health professional or a trusted friend. It makes for an interesting activity over coffee.

Self-Trusting Strategies	Actions
Explain how you can quietly reflect by journaling or meditating on your thoughts, feelings, and needs. This helps you identify your values, strengths, and triggers.	
Pay attention to your gut feelings and subtle inner nudges when you turn down the volume of your BPD. Describe your "right path" as best you can, even if you can't explain it logically.	
Embrace your strengths and weaknesses, along with any flaws and quirks. List the things that make you YOU. Don't strive for perfection but recognize that you inherently deserve love and respect. Write out what you can do or say to yourself that shows you accept your whole self.	
Write out the loudest negative thoughts that pop into your head and challenge their validity. Are they based on truth, BPD fallacy, or past experiences?	
Challenge your negative self by writing positive affirmations of self-compassion. Instead of saying *I'm a failure*, tell yourself *I made a mistake, but I can learn and grow from it.*	

Self-Trusting Strategies	Actions
Allow yourself forgiveness and move on. Don't dwell on the past or punish yourself for past failures. Write out your mistakes, then crumble it up and throw it away. It's time to move on. Describe how this felt.	
Build your confidence and trust through completing simple tasks and then celebrate your successes. What simple tasks can you do and take notice of that you completed well?	
Try new things, even if they feel scary. Facing your fears and achieving the unexpected boosts your confidence. What new healthy things can you try?	
Identify your natural talents and areas of expertise. Write out how you'll develop and utilize these strengths to feel competent and empowered.	
Surround yourself with positive and encouraging people who believe in you and lift you up. List who can you reach out to and what you can do to strengthen that connection.	

This is great! You started your journey to build trust in yourself. This is an important step, as this will help you nurture this part of yourself. Go back to these strategies and actions to help build trust with your FP.

TRUSTING YOUR FP

It can be exceptionally difficult to trust someone else with your heart, secrets, and other aspects of your life, especially when BPD is present. However, building the foundation of a relationship you can feel comfortable in requires a good sense of trust. The three building blocks to trusting your FP are reliability, respect, and vulnerability. The exercise below is going to help you broaden your perspective and hopefully enhance your comfort with these critical pieces of trust.

CONNECTING TO AND TRUSTING MY FP

You can boost your connection to your FP by creating an action plan using the building trust strategies you'll outline below. This may not be easy, and you may feel overwhelmed. If you feel this way, take a break and come back to it. It'll be here when you're ready. Think of this as an exciting experiment, not a frightening task. Remember, the goal is to build connection and trust, so don't feel like you must develop a perfect action plan. You need to create an action plan that fits you. Perfection is not needed.

If you need more space, grab a sheet of paper, your journal, or type it out in your phone. Also, if you get stuck, use your FP as a resource to help you write your actions down. This can be a great intimacy-building exercise, along with all the others throughout this workbook.

Building Trust Strategies	Actions
Describe how you can follow through on commitments, promises, and deadlines and show that you can be counted on.	
Explain how you can be there for your FP when they need you and offer help and support even when it's inconvenient.	

Building Trust Strategies	Actions
List ways you can maintain a consistent level of communication, support, and reliability over time.	
Describe your boundaries and how each of you can communicate and define your perspective.	
Write out how you can appreciate, consider, and trust others' thoughts and feelings, even if you don't always agree.	
Describe how you can offer gentle reminders of their goals, their strengths, and their reasons for joining you on this journey. What can you do to help them navigate any doubts or setbacks with unwavering belief.	
Describe how you can slowly show your FP who you really are, your vulnerabilities and strengths. This helps to foster deeper connection and trust.	
Explain how you can take responsibility for your actions and apologize when you're wrong. Remember, don't blame or make excuses.	
Describe what helps you take constructive criticism and feedback and use them as opportunities to learn and grow.	

Exercises like these tend to build a lot of insight, but they can also tap into core content issues and trigger your BPD. If that happened, it's not a bad thing, but an understandable response to addressing trust and helping it grow. Now that you're armed with your building trust action plan, it's time to continue your process of growth and understanding in your relationship foundation. The next section is going to continue to build on the concepts you've learned so far and help you feel comfortable discussing your wants and needs, both physically and emotionally, with confidence and positivity.

Openly Explore Your Emotional and Physical Desires

Your BPD likely convinced you that your emotional and physical wants are wrong or shameful, that having these desires makes you "weird" or bad. That's not true. Wanting emotional and physical closeness is part of being human. In healthy, consensual relationships, these desires are a way to share yourself. When you feel safe and open, they can even be fun.

It's okay to enjoy your body and feel close to someone you care about. If your FP is a family member or someone non-romantic, it might feel awkward to talk about this with them. That's completely normal. You can talk instead with a therapist, a healthy friend, or even just start by being honest with yourself, without shame.

Don't skip this section. Understanding your desires helps you feel calmer and more confident. The exercise below will help you get more comfortable with your body and express what you want. It takes time, like breaking in a new pair of fancy shoes. At first, they feel tight and strange, but the more you wear them, the better they fit. That's how this process works. Be patient with yourself. Keep walking, you'll get there.

12 REFLECTIONS TO EMOTIONAL AND PHYSICAL CLARITY

The twelve prompts below are designed to help you explore your needs and wants. They're not all about sex, as our wants and desires are often about connection to others, and not always physical connection. Respond to each prompt as honestly and clearly as you can. Don't judge yourself and don't let your BPD make you feel bad about wanting emotional and physical closeness. If this is too challenging, you may want help completing this, and a trusted mental health provider can be a great resource. You can answer it with a close friend, too. It may be enlightening to hear their answers as well.

1. Describe your thoughts and feelings about sex or someone touching you.

    _____

    _____

    _____

2. In what way do you like someone to touch you (softly, light rubbing, and so on)?

    _____

    _____

    _____

3. Write out your ideal talk about your physical needs and wants.

    _____

    _____

    _____

4. When we're intimate, I'd like you to _____

    _____

    _____

5. My fantasy is _____

    _____

    _____

6. I feel more confident we're close when you _____

    _____

    _____

7. I imagine me initiating sex by doing (write a start, middle, and end to your sequence)

    _____

    _____

    _____

8. I can show my body love by _____

_____

_____

9. I'm confused by my sexuality due to _____

_____

_____

10. Being open to new physical experiences would look like _____

_____

_____

11. I'd like to learn more about (add topic of interest, e.g., tantra, Kamasutra, and so on).

_____

_____

_____

12. Describe your next steps to physical closeness with yourself and others.

_____

_____

_____

This was likely not an easy exercise to complete. I'm super proud of you for doing your best and being willing to examine a topic that is sensitive for most people, but particularly so for those with BPD, as physical closeness can be confusing and scary. Certainly, desires and needs are a big part of any relationship, but ruptures in a connection are going to happen. Let's go build skills to go from disagreements to discussions.

From Disagreements to Discussions

Your BPD likes to immobilize you with fear, leading to the tendency to further complicate any situation that activates your underlying core content of abandonment, rejection sensitivity, emptiness, or whatever specific core content you may have. Disagreements can be minor or major, but your BPD takes advantage of you and the instance that caused the rupture in the relationship, which drives you to turn on yourself. Well, that was then, this is now.

Disagreements are a natural part of life and relationships, especially with those closest to you, like your FP. While they can be frustrating and frightening, they also present opportunities for growth and understanding. The steps outlined below are to help you learn how to manage these moments, then you'll personalize the steps by completing the worksheet that follows.

The Eight Steps to Resolution

Below is the list of steps to guide you through your disagreements. Read through them, then complete the worksheet that follows. Change is about learning, but it's also about putting this learning into action, just like you'll do here.

1. **Stay in the Moment—Recognize!** When you feel your heart rate increase, your stomach tighten, and your perspective narrow, pay attention to these and other biological markers that a disagreement has occurred. This is your brain and body telling you that you've been activated, more specifically that your core content has been activated. Stay present, and *don't react* using old maladaptive destructive behaviors.

2. **Cool Down and Calm Down:** Resist diving into the heat of the argument, take a step back and cool down. Give yourself some time to process your emotions and avoid acting impulsively. Take a few deep breaths, go for a walk, or do whatever helps you calm down and approach the situation with a clear head. Your BPD is going to further amplify your core content. Don't let it. Stay separate from whatever activated you, your FP, the topic, and so on, until you calm down. You may need to go for a run, exercise, scream into a pillow, and that is totally fine. The critical component of this step is to not act on the core content activation.

3. **The Right Place and Time:** Don't try to resolve the disagreement when you're both still fuming or in a crowded, public place. Find a quiet, private space where you can talk openly and honestly without distractions. You may need to set ground rules of keeping your distance, no throwing things, no name-calling, and so on. If you can't seem to reach

a mutually calm place, take another break and go back to step one until you are. It's ok to take a step back, we all must do it sometimes.

4. **Listen Actively:** Avoid interrupting or talking over each other and practice active listening. Remember what you learned earlier in the section Listening and Feeling Heard. It's time to use what you've learned and pay attention to what your FP is saying. Try to understand their perspective and avoid making assumptions. Show that you're genuinely interested in hearing their point of view.

5. **Communicate Respectfully:** Avoid using blame, insults, or personal attacks. Stick to the issue at hand and express your feelings in a respectful and assertive way. If either of you go off track, that's ok, say "I think we're getting off track, let's take a moment." Use "I" statements to focus on your own feelings and experiences, rather than accusing the other person.

6. **Focus on Common Ground:** Don't overly focus on your differences. Try to find common ground. Look for areas where you agree, even if they're small. This helps build the trust you're working toward, and it fosters a positive environment for seeking solutions.

7. **Be Willing to Compromise:** No one is going to get everything they want in a disagreement. Remember, we talked about probability and not guarantees. This is putting that to work for you. Be willing to compromise and find a solution that works for both of you. It's a give and take. Resist the urge to split (we discussed this concept in chapter 1), as this gives BPD the opportunity to turn healthy compromise into an "I must win at all costs" fallacy. Be flexible and open to considering your and your FP's needs and wants.

8. **Seek Help If Needed:** If you're struggling to resolve the disagreement, don't hesitate to seek help from a neutral third party, such as a mediator or therapist. They can provide guidance and support in facilitating communication and finding a solution. This doesn't mean the relationship is doomed. It means you need some help, and that's ok. Finding a neutral party, like a therapist, takes effort, but it can be crucial for the well-being of the relationship, and for each of you individually.

ACTION STEPS TO DISAGREEMENT RESOLUTION

Remember, resolution of disagreements is a continuous process, not a one-time event. It takes time, patience, and a willingness to work together. By writing out your personalized approach and following these steps, you can turn disagreements that amplify your relationship problem areas into opportunities for growth to strengthen your relationships. Consider your top three relationship problem areas and how you can use the steps to de-escalate issues and response patterns associated with them.

See the worksheet at http://www.newharbinger.com/56050 for examples of what Barbara did and said at each step. You can do the same things she did, or come up with your own steps that work best for you.

Working through disagreements is an ongoing journey that demands dedication, understanding, and cooperation. Remember, the process involves time, patience, and a genuine willingness to work together. By incorporating the steps you outlined above, you're adding to your flexibility and options when barriers occur and relationship problem areas surface. The more you practice these steps and communicate clearly, the easier it gets to turn challenges into chances to grow closer and build a stronger relationship with your FP.

Setting the Stage for Relationship Success

Using the spaces below, pull together what you learned from this chapter so you can take this information with you and use it in your relationships.

How will the skills you've learned in this chapter help you manage your top three BPD relationship problem areas?

_____

_____

_____

_____

In what ways can the skills you've learned in this chapter help you respond more calmly to disagreements or feedback?

_____

_____

_____

_____

What skills can you apply from this chapter to have greater mood stabilization and maintain consistency in your relationship?

_____

_____

_____

_____

What can you use from this chapter to build a close relationship with your FP?

_____

_____

_____

_____

How can the skills you've learned in this chapter help you increase trust, acceptance, and love in your relationship?

_____

_____

_____

_____

We're now going to further build on what you've learned and see how it fits and impacts various types of relationships. Understanding this and how these types impact your view and relationships will further strengthen your ability to successfully maneuver and balance variations of closeness.

CHAPTER 4

Dynamics and Barriers to Relationship Closeness

Individuals with BPD often try to manage their vulnerability to emotional closeness in relationships through a variety of maladaptive patterns learned over years of painful experiences, disappointments, and disillusionments reinforced by BPD. Sometimes, when you're trying really hard to get close to someone, the fear of them leaving or rejecting you takes over. To protect yourself, you might do things, like being too clingy or pulling away, that actually make them feel pushed away, amplifying your relationship problem areas. Even though you're trying to keep the connection, your actions can end up making it harder for them to stay close. It may feel like you engage in these patterns instinctively to protect you from getting hurt, but in reality, it's the BPD paradox, discussed in the introduction, that's likely at work causing an increase in the probability of relationship problems or destruction.

Let's take a look at Lonnie and his relationship with Sunny to illustrate how maladaptive relationship dynamics, barriers, and emotional patterns work against the probability of relationship happiness.

• Cloudy Skies for Lonnie and Sunny

Lonnie is 29 years old and was diagnosed with BPD when he was 19. As he has gotten older, he has become more frustrated with not finding "the one" who is going to make him feel safe, loved, and in emotional control. Lonnie met Sunny at the grocery store. They both have a love for exotic foods, and this common interest grew from a friendship into a romantic relationship. As their relationship developed, Lonnie found himself feeling increasingly dependent on Sunny, his FP. For Lonnie, Sunny represents all those things "the one" is supposed to bring to a turbulent sea of emotions. Every day, Lonnie's need for Sunny's full attention intensifies. He constantly checks his phone for messages, and any delay in response sends him spiraling into intense worry and imagined rejection. This causes him to "blow up" her phone with calls and texts to try and get reassurance she's still in love with him.

With so much time and energy going to verify Sunny's feelings, he stopped contacting his best friend Paul, and his mom noticed he was not reaching out to his sisters and grandma like he used to. Knowing his tendency to over-rely on others, particularly women, for emotional support and to neglect his own needs, she worried. But the more she reached out, the less he would accept her calls or discuss his relationship with Sunny.

When Lonnie and Sunny would go out, he would stay close to her, his eyes tracking every interaction she had with someone else, whether it's a "hello" or even a "thank you" to a restaurant server. He logs into her social media accounts without her knowledge and removes those he did not want her to associate with, mostly men. Lonnie often accuses her of not loving him enough and not caring about their relationship. With each scrap of attention Lonnie doesn't get, a tightness grows in his chest. This dependency is exhausting for both of them, but Lonnie feels powerless to stop it and feels he can't clearly discuss it with her. He vacillates between idolizing Sunny for her caring nature and resenting her for not always being available. These issues strain their relationship, leaving Lonnie to navigate his intense emotions along with the fear of losing her, his FP. Over time, Sunny feels pressure and uncertainty about the relationship as Lonnie's changing moods and behaviors cause her to feel confused and question if they can find a stable foundation in which to have the loving relationship they both want.

Lonnie and Sunny have several relationship dynamics and barriers in place that decrease the probability of relationship success. As you went through the story, did you identify similar dynamics and barriers that are present in your relationship with your FP? If you could, that's a great start. If you couldn't, that's ok too, because you're going to build this insight and knowledge as you go through this chapter.

This chapter will help you expand how you see and understand your relationships, giving you more control and better chances for success. As you go through it, you'll reflect on how certain factors affect your relationships and the problem areas you've already identified. You'll look at how different roles change your relationship and how that can help or hurt things.

This reflection will help you see if your relationships have improved, gotten more confusing, or made problems worse. You'll also explore what gets in the way of closeness and why. Let's begin by looking at the different types of relationships and how they connect to your life.

Your Relationship Types

Not all relationships are the same, but you're likely drawn to certain types based on your past. These past experiences, good, bad, painful, or scary, helped create a blueprint in your mind for what kind of relationship you think you "deserve." The word "deserve" is in quotes because it's what BPD has told you you're worth, often weighted toward the negative. You may have taken that message in without realizing it, and now it's hard to see other, healthier possibilities that could help you grow and feel stronger.

In this chapter, we'll look at a range of relationship types, from healthy to harmful. Some may feed your BPD patterns, but others won't. You might notice you have different types of relationships with different people, and that's okay. That variety can actually be a sign of progress and can help you better understand how BPD shows up in your life.

Based upon the severity of your BPD symptoms and traits, you're likely to have some adaptive and some maladaptive relationships based upon the closeness or intimacy you feel with the other person in the relationship. If your BPD symptoms are mild or moderate in severity, it's likely you have several relationship types based upon the context and degree of intimacy that's present. For example, you may have more of an adaptive relationship type at work, due to low intimacy likelihood, but at home with your FP it's more maladaptive, because of the high intimacy likelihood. This variability indicates that you're able to adjust your relationships based upon the person, context, closeness, and so on. On the other side of the spectrum, if your BPD symptoms are severe or extreme, you're more likely to have one, maybe two, relationship types and you try and force everyone in your life into them, including your FP. In these instances, intimacy is perceived to be high or intense, as you feel a strong possibility of threat, abandonment, rejection, and so on. In this case, relationships tend to be extreme and manifest as people feel pressured to be in the "right" relationship with you while you feel as though they're not doing enough to help you feel safe and secure. Let's look at Lonnie to add more clarification.

Lonnie, struggling with severe BPD, often forces those around him into a codependent and toxic type of relationship. His need for constant reassurance and validation manifests in relentless texting, checking, and various maladaptive tactics to see if others are still there, still care, and are accepting of him. This dynamic creates a maladaptive cycle where Lonnie's fears of abandonment are continually reinforced, leaving everyone involved feeling emotionally drained and unable to establish healthier, more balanced connections with him.

Lonnie engages in these behaviors using the BPD paradox. He is trying to reassure himself of something his BPD is telling him he'll never get, so he engages in maladaptive beliefs, behaviors, and patterns to try and reach his goals of emotional safety, but these processes cause the opposite, creating distance between him and those in his life. You may have been or are in the same spot as Lonnie, but we're gonna do this differently and broaden your relationship understanding to give you the power of choice. So, let's get started.

The first exercise in this chapter will help you identify the types of relationships you have and the factors that influence them. This exercise is the initial step in creating a framework to improve your understanding and perspective on relationships. It aims to empower you to see your relationships more clearly and understand the factors that contribute to negative outcomes.

Your Relationship Types and Influencers

The seven relationship types are composed of maladaptive, vague, and adaptive types. There is a blank box at the end of this exercise in case you have a relationship type that's not listed; be sure to include a description of this relationship type along with the name you have for it if you use this box. After you've reviewed the relationship types, rank in order your relationship types based on the frequency in which you're in them, from Always to Never.

As you complete this exercise, don't overly focus on the person or people in your life yet as they are likely to skew your objectivity, allowing BPD to confuse the process. You only want to explore the relationship types you tend to get into and the factors that influence these relationships. You may be asking, why not include specific people? BPD is highly influenced by people and the level of intimacy you have with them. But people aren't the only influencing components, and it's important to be able to see your relationships without these confusing additives.

The Relationship Types

Abusive (maladaptive)	Physical, emotional, sexual, and/or psychological harm is inflicted by you or your partner onto the other.
Codependent (maladaptive)	Excessive emotional or psychological reliance on your partner, often at the expense of yours or their own needs or well-being.
Toxic (maladaptive)	Behavior that is harmful to one or both of you, such as constant conflict, disrespect, manipulation, withholding, or not providing support.
Ambiguous (vague)	You feel uncertainty and a lack of clear direction as to where you stand and where the relationship is going and how each partner feels about the other.
Respectful and Equal (adaptive)	You respect each other's boundaries, values, and independence. Decisions are made together, reflecting fairness and mutual respect.
Communicative and Trustworthy (adaptive)	Open and honest communication is central, allowing each of you to express your thoughts and feelings safely. Trust is deeply established, without jealousy or suspicion.
Supportive and Growth-Producing (adaptive)	You support each other's personal and mutual growth, offering encouragement and understanding. You both handle conflicts constructively, fostering a positive and nurturing environment.

Use the spaces below to rank the relationship types you experience, from "Always" to "Never." These rankings should reflect the types of relationships you typically find yourself in across all contexts. Take a look at Lonnie's list first to help you. He considered a variety of relationships, such as those at work, school, romantic relationships, family connections, and others.

1. Always Codependent

2. Very Often Toxic

3. Often Ambiguous

4. Sometimes Respectful and equal

5. Rarely Supportive and growth-producing

6. Seldom Abusive

7. Never Communicative and trustworthy

By doing this exercise, Lonnie was able to see that his relationships always have an overreliance on getting his partner's emotional or psychological needs met while sacrificing his own needs and wellbeing. This creates a sense of resentment in him, as he feels sacrificed and irrelevant due to his codependency. He also recognized that he never feels as though his relationships have sincere communication and a sense of safety to where he feels open about his thoughts and emotions.

It's your turn to put in your rankings. Don't worry if this is hard at first; that's an expected response as this is something new. Just do your best and you can always redo it as many times as you need to. It's paper and pencil and not set in stone. You can use extra paper if you need to, or you can download a copy of this exercise at http://www.newharbinger.com/56050.

1. Always _____

2. Very Often _____

3. Often _____

4. Sometimes _____

5. Rarely _____

6. Seldom _____

7. Never _____

Now you're going to take this information with you as you explore those factors that impact your relationships.

THE RELATIONSHIP INFLUENCERS

Below is a list of influencing factors that likely play an important part in creating one or more of the above relationship types in your life. As you review these factors, think about the relationship types you listed above and how these factors increase and decrease the likelihood of one relationship type over another. Use the list below to identify the factors that affect how often you experience certain types of relationships. For example, if you're always in toxic relationships, it might be because of a lack of respect, shared interests, fairness, or empathy. The factors below are there to help you understand what's contributing to that type of relationship and how often it occurs.

Influential Factors	
☐ **Shared Interests:** Enjoying similar activities.	☐ **Work Environment:** The culture and atmosphere in the workplace.
☐ **Reliability:** Consistently keeping commitments and being dependable.	☐ **Team Dynamics:** The level of collaboration and teamwork.
☐ **Support:** Providing help in times of need.	☐ **Leadership Style:** Approachability and influence of leaders.
☐ **Fun:** Sharing laughter and enjoyable experiences.	☐ **Transparency:** Being open, honest, and authentic to build trust and understanding in relationships.
☐ **Respect:** Valuing opinions and differences.	☐ **Recognition and Rewards:** Appreciation and incentives for efforts.
☐ **Intimacy:** Emotional and physical closeness.	☐ **Commitment:** Dedication to maintaining the relationship.
☐ **Romantic Compatibility:** Alignment of romantic interests.	☐ **Life Goals:** Shared future plans and aspirations.
☐ **Time Spent Together:** Quantity and quality of shared time.	☐ **Family Roles:** Clarity and acceptance of responsibilities within the family.

Influential Factors	
☐ **Parenting Style:** Views on raising children.	☐ **Shared Responsibilities:** Division of household tasks.
☐ **Family Traditions:** Rituals and customs practiced by the family.	☐ **Community Engagement:** Participation in community activities.
☐ **Social Norms:** Adherence to community standards.	☐ **Diversity and Inclusion:** Acceptance of differences.
☐ **Networking Opportunities:** Social and professional connections available.	☐ **Communication:** Quality and clarity of interactions.
☐ **Trust:** Dependability and honesty.	☐ **Fairness:** Treating each other equally and considering both people's needs.
☐ **Shared Values:** Common beliefs and priorities.	☐ **Empathy:** Understanding and sharing others' feelings.
☐ **Conflict Resolution:** Methods of addressing disagreements.	☐ **Compatibility:** Alignment of personalities and interests.
☐ **Emotional Support:** Offering understanding, encouragement, and care during both good and difficult times.	☐ **Compassion:** Showing kindness and a genuine desire to help and understand others.

This exercise is going to ask you to identify the relationship types you're "Always," "Very often," and "Often" in and the influential factors that support or encourage that relationship type. Before you get started, let's take a look at Lonnie's top three most frequent relationship types and the factors that influence them.

My always Codependent relationship type is influenced by (add influential factors) absence of trust, communication, intimacy, commitment, compatibility, and support.

My very often Toxic relationship type is influenced by (add influential factors) absence of fairness, reliability, emotional support, lack of mutual trust, compassion, and dedication and interest in me.

My often Ambiguous relationship type is influenced by (add influential factors) absence of transparency, fairness, and emotional and practical support in times of need.

When we take a step back, as Lonnie did, he was able to see that his top three types are negative and filled with absence of support, caring, trust, compassion, and other factors. These are issues Lonnie feels within his relationships without considering the person he's in the relationship with. This was shocking to him, as he always believed, and his BPD reinforced this with maladaptive beliefs, behaviors, and patterns, that it was the other person who caused these factors and feelings to exist. Seeing this helped Lonnie understand that if these are things inside him, he can have more control over them.

It's your turn. Complete the sections below and do your best not to think about a specific person or people.

My always _____ relationship type is influenced by (add influential factors)

_____

_____

My very often _____ relationship type is influenced by (add influential factors)

_____

_____

My often _____ relationship type is influenced by (add influential factors)

_____

_____

List the common influencers you notice across your top three relationship types:_____

_____

_____

_____

_____

_____

Completing the above exercise without considering any specific individual was likely challenging, but it enhanced your ability to be objective. It helped you see your relationships and the factors that influence them beyond just the people involved. This is a huge step in clarifying your relationship dynamics. The more you see those types and factors, the more you build insight and can learn strategies, like those in this workbook, to manage them, which gives you power to control your BPD and resist the tendency to distort how you see yourself, others, and the world around you.

For the next step, we're going to explore the *what* and the *how*, adding to your insight to build a better understanding of the way your relationships change as your intimacy builds.

Understanding Your Relationship Roles

Relationship roles help you understand and manage how close you are to others. Different people in your life play different roles, depending on the situation. BPD can make these roles feel confusing and leave you feeling powerless, like you're just being pulled along by life, crashing into problems you can't avoid. This often comes from past experiences where you didn't feel like you had control in relationships. But you can learn to guide your path. In this section, we'll explore your relationship roles and how they affect your connections, so you can avoid the "rocks" and reduce relationship problems.

Intimacy is key to understanding these roles. Emotional, physical, and intellectual closeness makes some relationships, like romantic partners, your FP, best friends, or close family, deeper and more complex. These connections require more emotional effort and often impact your well-being the most, especially if you struggle with BPD patterns.

Other relationships, like with coworkers or acquaintances, have lower intimacy and are usually simpler. By learning how intimacy levels shape each role, you can manage expectations better, build healthier relationships, and feel more in control of your connections.

The "What" and the "How"

Below is a list of nine relationship roles along with definitions to help you identify the various positions people have in your life, such as friends, family, colleagues, and romantic partners. The list is structured based on the degree of intimacy you're likely to have with someone in that role. It begins with people you know but don't spend much time with and progresses to those you may commit to spending your life with. Your FP is very likely to fall into one of the more intimate roles, meaning emotionally close but not necessarily sexual.

Roles
1.   **Acquaintances:** These are casual contacts, familiar faces you see in passing.
2.   **Colleagues:** Coworkers or people in your professional sphere.
3.   **Casual Friends:** These are occasional companions you share hobbies or interests with.
4.   **Mentor/Mentee:** Someone who offers guidance and support to another's development.
5.   **Casual Dating:** Non-exclusive romantic relationships where you get to know each other without a long-term commitment.
6.   **Close Friends:** These are friends that offer trust, support, and a deep connection.
7.   **Romantic Partners:** These are people or a person you share love, intimacy, and commitment with.
8.   **Committed Partners:** Long-term romantic relationships, which may include living together, sharing significant life decisions, and often planning for the future together.
9.   **Family:** These are relatives, important others, or chosen loved ones who you have a deep connection with and a lasting bond.

As you went through the list, you may not have someone in your life in every role. It's okay if you don't, and don't let your BPD make you feel deficient because of this. You're not deficient; you simply don't have people in every role, and that's just fine.

It may have been overwhelming to try to think of everyone in your life in those various roles. You may've missed some, and that's fine. You can always come back and reconsider their role any time. To make the most of this exercise, let's focus on the top three most intimate relationship roles. Your FP will certainly be in there, but if your FP is composed of more than one individual, you can add those people into numbers 2 and 3 below too.

Who's in What Role. Let's first take a look at Lonnie's responses to further clarify the next steps. Sunny is his FP, but his mom, sisters, and grandma, as well as Paul are also very significant people in his life. So, he had to add them as well into his top three.

1.   I would put Sunny (FP) as falling into the Romantic Partner role.

2. I would put Mom, Maddy (sister), Carol (sister), and Grandma Ruth (FP) as falling into the Family role.

3. I would put Paul (FP) as falling into the Close Friend role.

By completing this exercise, Lonnie was able to see where these individuals fall within his life, but more importantly, he recognized that those roles are ones that have a high degree of intimacy, which alerts him that BPD is most likely to severely disrupt these relationships.

Now it's your turn to complete the blanks below. You can use extra paper if you need to, or you can download a copy of this exercise at http://www.newharbinger.com/56050.

1. I would put _____ (FP) as falling into the _____ role.

2. I would put _____ (FP) as falling into the _____ role.

3. I would put _____ (FP) as falling into the _____ role.

Great job! This is likely a different way to perceive individuals and the roles they occupy in your life, but we're not done yet. I want you to take another step so you can see the change that occurs when you consider the role, without emphasis on the specific person, and *how* the relationship transforms.

The How. The roles people play in your life and how close you are to them can have a big impact on your relationships. Without even noticing, you may react in certain ways because of how important someone is to you or how close you feel to them. The closer the relationship, the more likely it is to bring out beliefs, behaviors, and patterns connected to BPD. By understanding how these roles and degrees of intimacy affect you, you can start to see how your relationship problem areas often feel out of control and difficult to manage. Remember, this does not mean impossible. Just like Lonnie, increasing your insight will help you be more aware of BPD's maladaptive influence.

The exercise below will help you explore how the roles people play in your life and the level of closeness you share with them impact your BPD-related beliefs, behaviors, and patterns and your relationship problem areas. By breaking down these relationships step-by-step, you can see how your emotions, reactions, and struggles are connected to a specific role and the related relationship's intimacy. Building this insight encourages reflection on how these factors make certain problem areas better, worse, or stay the same, helping you have greater control over your triggers and how BPD influences your relationships.

For the first part of this exercise, think about the person you listed above. This might be your FP, and the role they play in your life. Next, identify your top three relationship problem areas and consider whether having this person in that role makes those problems better, the same, or worse. For example, if Sunny is Lonnie's romantic partner, does that help make the problems better, worse and harder to deal with, or have no real impact? Then, describe how that person's role in your life affects the relationship problem areas. Finally, think about how much of the influence comes from the person specifically and how much comes from the role they play in your life. Give each one a percentage, and make sure the two numbers add up to 100 percent. Also, consider how your BPD and intimacy adds to the challenges in managing these dynamics. Take your time to reflect and be honest with yourself as you work through these steps. Let's look at Lonnie's updated responses using his high intimate relationship roles.

Identify the role: Write the name of the person and their role in your life below (e.g., parent, close friend, romantic partner).

Sunny, romantic partner

Relationship problem areas: List the relationship problem areas that are impacted by this role. Focus on the role itself, rather than the person. Then, think about how that role affects the relationship problem area. Is the problem area better, worse, or the same when interacting with that role? Note its effect on the right.

1. Frequent fear of abandonment   Worse

2. Excessive clinginess or neediness   Same

3. Extreme jealousy and control issues   Worse

Connect to patterns: Describe how the relationship problem areas are made better, worse, or the same by that role and how your BPD makes it more difficult.

My romantic partner makes my fear of abandonment worse by not always responding quickly, triggering my intense worry, and my jealousy gets worse when she's friendly to others, which I see as threatening. Her caring nature keeps my clinginess the same by reassuring me. My BPD amplifies these issues with extreme, split views, idolizing my romantic partner when I feel loved and resenting her when I fear rejection. These patterns reflect my past tendency to over-rely on others for emotional stability, repeating unhealthy cycles in relationships.

How much of the influence is based on the person, as compared to the role they occupy in your life? Put two percentages but make sure they equal 100 percent.

Specific Person	Role They Occupy
10%	90%

Now that you've seen how Lonnie completed this exercise, it's your turn. Take your time and you can use extra paper if you need to, or you can download a copy of this exercise at http://www.newharbinger.com/56050.

Identify the role: Write the name of a person and their role in your life below (e.g., parent, close friend, romantic partner).

_____

_____

Relationship problem areas: List the relationship problem areas that are impacted by this role. Focus on the role itself, rather than the person. Then, think about how that role affects the relationship problem area. Is the problem area better, worse, or the same when interacting with that role? Note its effect on the right.

1. _____   _____

2. _____   _____

3. _____   _____

Connect to patterns: Describe how the relationship problem areas are made better, worse, or the same by that person being in that role and how your BPD makes it more difficult.

_____

_____

_____

_____

How much of the influence is based on the person, as compared to the role they occupy in your life? Put two percentages but make sure they equal 100 percent.

Specific Person	Role They Occupy

Doing this exercise helped Lonnie realize that it wasn't specifically Sunny, or his individual family members or close friends who contributed to making his relationship problem areas worse. It was the high-intimacy roles they played in his life. This made his connections to those with whom he was closest more confusing and threatening. This powerful insight prepared him to take the next steps in exploring barriers to closeness.

Bringing all of these relationship factors together helps you gain critical insight into how the roles people occupy in your life impact your relationships and your perspective of them. It's not always the person, but the role they occupy that activates your BPD beliefs, behaviors, and patterns that influence your relationship problem areas. This understanding is crucial for managing your relationships in a more adaptive way. Let's now explore the barriers that prevent you from achieving the intimacy and closeness you desire.

My Barriers to Closeness

Individuals with BPD often contend with the push and pull of wanting to be close while being afraid of the closeness due to fear of abandonment and rejection, which leads to emptiness. This maladaptive self-protective response often manifests in various barriers between you and your FP causing your relationship to feel unsafe. Barriers impact the closeness of your relationship by adding to your sense of feeling distant, lost, empty, alone, unsupported, and so on. These feelings and perspectives give your BPD power to influence how you see yourself, your relationships, your FP, and your world. To lessen the maladaptive impact of your BPD, you have to first identify your barriers and their impact on your relationship. This is similar to your previous task where you assessed roles, relationship types, and their influencers. The following exercise will help you apply these skills to barriers by first identifying your obstacles to intimacy.

Identifying Your Barriers to Closeness

BPD can make it hard to know what you really want in a relationship, what you think you deserve, and how close you can get before it all feels like it will fall apart. It often tricks you into believing that pain means love, keeping you on high alert all the time. This constant stress drains you, making it harder to think clearly and see how BPD is blocking you from getting your needs met, especially with your FP. To push back against these patterns, you need to strengthen your ability to recognize what's really going on. When you do, you'll have more energy to build healthier, more balanced relationships.

Below are six common relationship barriers. These happen in all relationships, not just those affected by BPD. But with BPD, you tend to use them more often as a way to protect yourself, which can actually harm the relationship instead of helping it.

Let's explore what these barriers are and look at how they've shown up in your relationships, so you can start changing how they affect you.

Barrier	Expression
Communication Issues	Misunderstandings, lack of openness, and poor listening skills prevent meaningful exchanges and mutual understanding.
Trust Issues	Past betrayals, dishonesty, or inconsistency impairs trust in each other, hindering closeness.
Emotional Unavailability	An inability to express or respond to emotions clearly, often adding confusion by sending distorted or mixed signals.
Fear of Vulnerability	The dread of exposing your true self and risking rejection or emotional hurt prevents you from forming deep, authentic connections.
Past Trauma	Unresolved issues from previous relationships or experiences can create emotional distance and encourage defensive behaviors.
Dependency/Control Issues	Stifles your relationship by creating an imbalanced dynamic where trust and independence cannot thrive, often leading to resentment.

As you read through these barriers, you likely recognized them appearing in your relationships, often seemingly without warning and to varying degrees. This happens because when you're in the heat of the moment and your BPD is activated by fear of abandonment, sensitivity to rejection, or feelings of emptiness, it can be very difficult to see the barrier coming before it manifests. Now that you know what these barriers are, you're ready to pair them with how they influence your relationship. To further illustrate, let's see Lonnie's barriers first (circled below), then it'll be your turn.

I see the following barriers in my relationships (circle all those that apply):

Barrier	
Communication Issues	(Fear of Vulnerability)
(Trust Issues)	Past Trauma
Emotional Unavailability	(Dependency/Control Issues)

These barriers add to my relationship being (circle all that apply):

Better   (More confusing)   (More ambiguous)   Worse

or add your own descriptor _____

This exercise helped Lonnie identify the specific barriers that exacerbate his relationship problem areas, allowing him to see how his relationships change based on the roles people have in his life. This insight not only added clarity and broadened his understanding of his relationships but also prepared him for uncovering the roots of his barriers and then how best to lessen BPD's adverse influence on his attempt to achieve genuine intimacy with those he values most. There are two spaces below for you to use, but if you need more you can use extra paper or you can download a copy of this exercise at http://www.newharbinger.com/56050.

I see the following barriers in my relationships (circle all those that apply):

Barrier	
Communication Issues	Fear of Vulnerability
Trust Issues	Past Trauma
Emotional Unavailability	Dependency/Control Issues

These barriers add to my relationship being (circle all that apply):

Better   More confusing   More ambiguous   Worse

or add your own descriptor _____

I see the following barriers in my relationships (circle all those that apply):

Barrier	
Communication Issues	Fear of Vulnerability
Trust Issues	Past Trauma
Emotional Unavailability	Dependency/Control Issues

These barriers add to my relationship being (circle all that apply):

Better   More confusing   More ambiguous   Worse

or add your own descriptor _____

You've been doing great work, and it's not easy uncovering dynamics and barriers to intimacy. There is one more step: identifying the roots to your barriers. Examining what lies beneath your barriers isn't easy, but it's essential. As you step away from the distorted lens of BPD (more about that in chapter 5) and apply the knowledge you've gained from this workbook, you can uncover the true drivers behind your barriers to closeness that negatively impact your relationship dynamics. This clarity will empower both you and your FP to navigate the challenges of BPD and your relationship problem areas related to insecurities and intimacy issues in your relationship.

Remember, there's a paradox in BPD: you crave connection, yet your barriers drive you to sabotage that closeness. We're going to break apart this painful protective paradox and infuse your relationship with harmony by building honest insight and managing your BPD contradiction.

Pare Down My Paradox of Protection

There are many possible reasons you use barriers to connection, and it's likely that you've developed these over time as protective measures. However, as you've gotten older, learned various skills, and enhanced your insight, you likely don't need these barriers any longer. BPD is a tricky adversary, and it knows to wed you to old protective strategies, so it gets empowered and continues its adverse influence on you and your relationship. The next exercise is going to explore the roots and reasons for your barriers so you can better understand why they're still in your life.

My Barrier Roots and Reasons

When you examine your barriers to closeness, can you identify their origins and the purpose they serve? It's likely that these barriers exist to keep you safe and prevent you from getting hurt. But go deeper, and ask yourself, *Safe from what?* Take some time to review and answer these insight-building questions to deepen your understanding of your relationship barriers to uncover their roots and impacts. Then, describe your reason for using them.

Getting to Roots and Reasons

What are my specific fears about getting emotionally close to someone?

_____

_____

What early experiences with attachment and bonding, especially with parents or caregivers, contributed to the creation of my relationship barriers?

_____

_____

Can you recall a situation where you felt fear of abandonment or rejection? What triggered it?

_____

_____

Where did I learn to use these barriers to closeness and why do I keep using them?

_____

_____

When and from whom did I learn to not depend on my FP or allow them to depend on me?

_____

_____

When I use my barriers, what do I hope will happen?

_____

_____

When my FP opens up to me, I feel (add emotions) and I learned this from (add in significant people from your past).

_____

_____

What specific behaviors do I exhibit when I feel threatened or vulnerable in a relationship?

_____

_____

How do my relationship barriers impact my ability to trust others?

_____

_____

Are there any recurring patterns in my relationships that suggest a fear of intimacy?

_____

_____

How do I typically react when someone tries to get close to me emotionally or physically?

_____

_____

What past experiences have reinforced my belief that maintaining these barriers is necessary?

_____

_____

I use my barriers to closeness because _____

_____

_____

Understanding these roots and reasons will empower you to be more honest with yourself and your FP. This self-awareness will enable you to integrate everything you've learned in this chapter to incorporate the following intimacy-building skills while resisting the urge to build barriers.

Building Intimacy While Blocking Maladaptive Patterns

Before we dive into comprehensive insight and skills, you may wonder what happened with Lonnie and Sunny. Lonnie realized his behaviors—constant texting, controlling actions, and emotional withdrawal—weren't helping him feel closer to Sunny. Instead, his BPD paradox was in charge, creating distance. After identifying his patterns and barriers, Lonnie committed to growing beyond his BPD and working on his relationship differently. Instead of reacting out of fear, he started asking himself questions like, _What am I afraid of?_ and _How can I communicate honestly instead?_ He soon discovered that by pausing and reflecting, he could replace controlling behaviors with healthy vulnerability and trust. For example, instead of blowing up Sunny's phone, he texted her once to say, _I'm feeling a little anxious right now, but I trust you'll get back to me when you can._ This shift made Sunny feel respected, which helped rebuild their connection. These and other behaviors helped him connect to Sunny but also made him feel better about himself and more in control of his beliefs, behaviors, and patterns.

Lonnie's work took time, but in the end, he found out that it was worth it, and it impacted many parts of his life, not just with Sunny, but with his family, friends, and coworkers. Now that you know your role, influencers, and other aspects of intimacy and related barriers, let's put it all together to help you go forward in an empowered way.

Using your earlier work in this chapter, identify the patterns that might harm intimacy.

What behaviors do you use to feel secure in relationships (example: "I over-text," "I avoid sharing my feelings," or "I try to control the other person's actions")?

_____

_____

_____

What emotions tend to drive these behaviors (e.g.. fear of abandonment, rejection, or not being enough)?

_____

_____

The next time you feel triggered, pause and ask yourself:

- *What am I really afraid of?*

   _____

   _____

- *What could I do instead that builds trust and respect?*

   _____

   _____

   You can do what Lonnie did as an example. The old pattern was to send ten texts when he didn't get an immediate reply. He replaced this with a new action: Send one text, then engage in a grounding activity like journaling or taking a walk.

Use the following strategies to lessen your relationship problem areas with honest intimacy that is built on communication, trust, and shared vulnerability.

Communicate clearly:

- **Instead of:** "You never care about me!"
- **Try:** "When I don't hear back from you, I feel worried. Can you let me know if you need more time?"

Acknowledge your emotions:

- Instead of hiding your feelings, name them.

  For example: "I'm feeling scared about how close we're getting because I really care about you."

Set healthy boundaries:

- Instead of checking someone's social media, remind yourself, *I want to trust them. If I feel uncertain, I'll talk to them directly instead.*

Incorporate these adaptive strategies into your daily routine. Remember, success is built into your daily routine, not in random moments.

Self-soothing before reacting:

- When you feel the urge to act out, pause and use a calming technique like deep breathing or grounding.

Reframe rejection as opportunity:

- **Instead of:** *They don't care about me.*
- **Try:** *This is a chance to reflect on what I need and say it clearly and kindly.*

Celebrate small wins:

- Acknowledge progress, no matter how small: *I only sent one text today instead of ten, and I felt proud of myself for practicing trust."*

Track positive changes:

- Use a journal or the workbook to help you recognize those positive changes. For example: *I noticed my partner smiles more when I share how I feel calmly.*

Recognize remaining challenges:

- Growth is an ongoing process, and issues will pop up from time to time. Build in understanding of ongoing challenges: *I still struggle with texting too much, but I'm learning to pause before reacting.*

Reframe rejection and missteps:

- **Instead of:** *They don't care about me.*
- **Try:** *This is a chance to learn and practice how I can communicate my needs more clearly.*

Reflecting on your relationship using these tools can be a powerful experience, helping you recognize how BPD's maladaptive influence detracts from your ability to get closer to those who matter most. Understanding what's in the way, and what, why, and how all of this relates to the functioning of your relationships will serve you well going forward. Take a moment to share these insights with your FP, if you feel comfortable, and encourage them to complete the online FP exercise for this chapter, "Defining Healthy and Unhealthy Interaction Patterns and Challenges in Relationships."

Setting the Stage for Relationship Success

Using the spaces below, pull together what you learned from this chapter so you can take this information with you and use it in your relationships.

How will the skills you've learned in this chapter help you manage your top three BPD relationship problem areas?

_____

_____

_____

_____

_____

In what ways can the skills you've learned in this chapter help you to better regulate your mood and maintain consistency in your relationship?

_____

_____

_____

_____

_____

What skills can you apply from this chapter to have greater mood stabilization and maintain consistency in your relationship?

_____

_____

_____

_____

What can you use from this chapter to build a close relationship with your FP?

_____

_____

_____

_____

How can the skills you've learned in this chapter help you increase trust, acceptance, and love in your relationship?

_____

_____

_____

_____

You have built your understanding of your relationship dynamics and barriers that impact your closeness and intimacy. In the next chapter, we're going to delve into how distorted perceptions of yourself, others, your FP, and your relationship dynamics can impact your interactions and overall well-being. We'll explore the origins of these distortions, their effects on your behavior and decisions, and provide strategies to recognize and correct them to foster healthier, more fulfilling relationships.

CHAPTER 5

Distorted Perceptions of Self, Other, and Relationship

The last four chapters helped you build a strong base for your relationships with your FP and others, which is important so you can start seeing your relationships more clearly, without the confusion that BPD causes. In this chapter, you're going to learn about how those distortions affect how you see yourself, others, your FP, and your relationships. There are different things that can cause these distortions, and by understanding them better, you'll be able to make better choices in your relationships and have greater control over your BPD relationship problem areas. The more disrupted your view of self is, the greater the likelihood of core content activation, which leads to expression of those BPD maladaptive beliefs, behaviors, perceptions, and patterns. This may have been helpful for you at one time, but as you've gotten older these maladaptive aspects have become even more distorted and more acidic, eroding your true view of self.

Before we dive into how you see yourself, let's meet Stacey, who will guide you through this chapter.

• Stacey's Journey from Distortion to Clarity

Stacey, a 34-year-old living in New York City and working in the fashion industry, has struggled with BPD since high school. She's single with no children but loves spending time with her nieces and nephews. Her BPD often distorts how she sees herself, making her feel unworthy, afraid of abandonment, and overly sensitive to rejection.

At work, Stacey feels isolated, convinced her coworkers focus on her flaws. These feelings have made it hard for her to keep jobs. For example, when her boss suggested using a lighter fabric for one of her designs, Stacey felt criticized and attacked. Overwhelmed, she lashed out, calling her boss a "jealous bitch," and was fired immediately.

In friendships, Stacey craves closeness but fears rejection if her friends see the "real" her. Once, during lunch with her friend Emily, Stacey grew anxious when Emily checked her phone several times. She assumed Emily was bored and uninterested, which left Stacey feeling tense and withdrawn for the rest of the meal.

Romantic relationships are another challenge. Stacey's fear of abandonment often leads to conflicts. When her boyfriend Paul was late for dinner due to traffic, she panicked. She didn't receive his texts explaining his delay because of poor cell service. When he arrived, Stacey accused him of not caring, bringing up past grievances. Even after Paul apologized, Stacey couldn't calm down, and the argument escalated, leading to them almost breaking up.

Stacey's biggest struggles are her fear of abandonment, clinginess, and tendency to withdraw when hurt. These patterns have made relationships difficult, but recognizing how her BPD impacts her thoughts and actions is helping her take steps toward healthier connections.

Stacey's reactions and perceptions are understandable for someone with BPD. BPD distorts how Stacey sees herself, others, and her relationships. It triggers her core feelings, making it harder for her to control her emotions and actions. Stacey's journey shows how tough it can be to deal with these distorted thoughts, but it also highlights the importance of getting help to learn better ways to cope. In this chapter, you'll see how Stacey worked to understand and manage her BPD distortions. Just like Stacey, your journey begins with understanding how you see yourself.

My BPD Lens

Your BPD lens distorts how you see things, like looking through a dark, tinted window that makes everything seem dim and negative. This distorted view makes you focus only on the bad parts of yourself, your life, and your relationship, affecting how you think and feel. Noticing this "tint" is the first step toward seeing a clearer picture, where you can appreciate both the good and the bad parts of reality. In this chapter, we'll explore how the BPD lens distorts your view of yourself and how it affects your relationships, intensifying your relationship problem areas.

The BPD lens makes you rely on negative thoughts, behaviors, and patterns to meet your needs and wants. While this might give you some quick relief, it often causes problems in the long run. Even though you might notice this, BPD pushes you to keep using this lens to get immediate satisfaction, which keeps the cycle going. By understanding how the BPD lens distorts your perception, you can start to challenge these false beliefs. This is an important step toward seeing yourself, others, and your relationships more clearly, recognizing both the positives and negatives instead of just focusing on the negative.

Seeing Clearly Without Your BPD Lens

To lessen the adverse influence of your BPD lens, we have to encourage your perspective without distortion. To begin, start by thinking about how you see yourself in tough moments when your feelings of abandonment, rejection, or emptiness take over. This is your BPD lens. Write down what you notice about yourself and how these feelings affect you. Then, consider how these feelings influence your top three relationship problem areas, like being overly clingy, avoiding people, or becoming defensive. Next, think about how these thoughts and behaviors keep you stuck in a negative cycle, making it harder to build healthy connections. Finally, challenge these negative views by looking for evidence of the truth, like Stacey did in the example below, to develop healthier beliefs and behaviors.

When I look at my relationships through my BPD lens, I see that I am alone, trapped, and waiting to be betrayed and rejected by the people I love.

Describe how this influences your top three BPD relationship problem areas: These feelings make my biggest relationship problems worse. My fears of being abandoned grow stronger, I become more needy, and I often feel like pulling away suddenly.

Due to seeing myself this way and how it impacts my relationship problems, I believe I am worthless, a terrible person, broken, and unlovable.

Because of this belief, I engage in the following behaviors that reinforce it: I tend to "test" people I care about, spying on where they go, bombarding them with questions about their feelings, thoughts, and intentions, and going through their phones when they're not looking.

My beliefs and behaviors support my dark, tinted lens because I notice that I often act in ways that show I don't trust others, and it causes arguments or problems. I think I'm protecting myself, but it actually makes me feel worse because I can't find enough proof to quiet the negative thoughts in my head. These actions make my relationships harder and add to my feelings of low self-worth, fear of being left out, and being too sensitive to rejection, emptiness, and failure.

This uncovering of her BPD lens' influence was just the start, but an important one, as she then learned that her true power is in refuting it, which you'll learn too in a moment.

Now it's your turn to dive into the first part. Try not to overthink your answers. Let them come from your true self, without the influence of your BPD lens. You may encounter one problem: You've been viewing life through this lens for so long that you've accepted it as truth. Just because you've believed something for so long doesn't make it true. This is a fallacy that has kept BPD in your life and your relationships for far too long. Time to challenge it!

When I look at my relationships through my BPD lens, I see that I am _____

_____

_____

Describe how this influences your top three BPD relationship problem areas: _____

_____

_____

_____

Due to seeing myself this way and how it impacts my relationship problems, I believe I am _____

_____

_____

_____

Because of this belief, I engage in the following behaviors that reinforce it: _____

_____

_____

_____

My beliefs and behaviors support my dark, tinted lens because I tend to engage in the following patterns:

_____

_____

_____

_____

The first part of this activity was likely very challenging, so be proud of yourself for getting through it. It helped you see how your BPD lens creates distortions of how you see yourself, others, your FP, and relationships. Let's push back even more on your BPD lens using the spaces below to refute it by providing evidence to support your truth versus BPD fallacy. Your responses must be based on what your true self sees and believes, the evidence in your life, not because your BPD says so. Stacey's first few answers have been provided to help get you started.

Refuting Your BPD Lens	
Stacey's Fallacy	**Stacey's Truth**
People only hang out with me to fool me into thinking they like me. Not everyone hangs out when I want to. My dad says I only get hired because of the way I look, not because of my skills.	People reach out to me often to hang out. I've gotten many jobs. People tell me they are impressed with my experience and hire me really quickly.
Your Fallacy	**Your Truth**

Below is a list of supportive relationship patterns to help you identify which ones might work best for you. In this exercise you're going to think about your top three relationship problem areas, identify one or two supportive relationship patterns, and then describe how using these patterns helps you see yourself and your FP more clearly and accurately. Before you get started, let's take a look at how Stacey approached this process.

Relationship problem area: Fear of abandonment leading to clinginess and overreacting to perceived rejection.

Supportive relationship patterns: Think before I react: When I start to feel upset, I'll pause, take a deep breath, and think about how I want to respond. Communicate clearly: I'll practice sharing my feelings in a clear and honest way, without blaming or becoming overly emotional.

How using the supportive relationship pattern helps you lessen your identified relationship problem area: Pausing before reacting helps me stay calm and I avoid jumping to conclusions or saying things I'll regret. Communicating clearly lets me share my feelings without blaming others. These patterns reduce misunderstandings and help me feel more secure in my relationships by being more authentic and helping me see issues and myself more clearly.

Now it's your turn. Choose one or two of the following supportive relationship patterns to help you complete the exercise below. You can use extra paper if you need to, or you can download a copy of this exercise at http://www.newharbinger.com/56050.

☐ **Think before I react:** When I start to feel upset, I'll pause, take a deep breath, and think about how I want to respond. This helps me stay calm and not say things I'll regret.

☐ **Be kind to myself:** I know it's okay to make mistakes. When things don't go perfectly, I'll remind myself that I can learn from it and move on, instead of being hard on myself.

☐ **Communicate clearly:** I'll practice sharing my feelings in a clear and honest way. It's important to say how I feel without blaming or getting too emotional.

☐ **Respect boundaries:** I'll pay attention to both my own boundaries and my FP's. If one of us needs space or time, I'll understand that it's normal and healthy.

☐ **Practice patience:** Relationships take time to grow. I'll remind myself that it's okay if everything isn't perfect right away, I'll keep trying and stay patient.

☐ **Focus on the good stuff:** Instead of getting stuck on negative things, I'll focus on what's going well and what I appreciate about myself and my FP. This will help me stay more positive.

Relationship problem area:_____

Supportive relationship patterns:_____

_____

_____

How using the supportive relationship pattern helps you lessen your identified relationship problem area:

_____

_____

_____

_____

_____

_____

Calling out your BPD lens, recognizing the truth in seeing yourself, others, your FP, and your relationship more authentically, and the influence supportive relationship patterns have over maladaptive ones hopefully make you feel empowered and positive about your ability to influence yourself and your relationship perceptions in a positive way, just like Stacey did. We're going to build on this and take a closer look at another challenge people with BPD face that affects relationships: an unstable self-image. This can make the top three relationship problems worse, often causing or adding even more strain.

My Fluctuating Self-Perception

Your BPD and unstable self-image probably started when you were a kid or teen. Things like your genes, your home life, or painful experiences, like being ignored, hurt, or made to feel like your feelings didn't matter, made it hard to build a strong sense of who you are. As you got older, you may have felt big emotions, changed your views often, or acted differently around different people to fit in or avoid rejection. This made it even harder to know your true self.

To cope, you may have taken on different "roles," which confused you more. This likely caused problems in close relationships, especially with your FP. Those relationships were probably full of ups and downs, making you feel empty, lost, or stuck. All this stress amplified your BPD. You may have acted on impulse, had emotional outbursts, or even hurt yourself to manage it but it often made things harder.

It can feel like you're standing on shaky ground, but learning to build a stable sense of self can help you feel confident about who you are, what matters to you, and where you're headed, while also helping you manage your BPD and relationship struggles.

You're not alone in this struggle. Stacey was there too.

Stacey often wondered who she really was, struggling with a shaky sense of self because of the invalidation and trauma she experienced growing up, which contributed to her BPD. As a child, her parents often brushed off her feelings, calling her too sensitive. In her teenage years, she experienced constant criticism at school, feeling like she could never be as good as her classmates. To cope, she started pretending to be different people to fit in, which led to chaotic relationships and a confused sense of who she was. At work, Stacey had a hard time making friends and often felt left out, which drove her to try even harder to fit in.

Wanting to find herself, Stacey started seeing a therapist to understand why she doubted herself so much. She learned how to see herself clearly and embrace her self-perception through exploration and challenging her self-perception in healthy ways. She also began doing things that really mattered to her. She kept a journal, writing about her past and how it shaped her. She signed up for a local art class, rediscovering her love for painting, which she hadn't done in years. This helped her feel more connected to who she truly was. Over time, Stacey weakened BPD's grip on her, gaining a more stable sense of self and building healthier relationships, weakening her problem areas. She was able to reconnect with old friends and make new ones based on respect and understanding. All of this provided her with a sense of stability that strengthened her relationship with her FP.

To stabilize your self-image, you'll start to identify the roots, followed by engagement in activities that'll help you recreate your sense of self into who you want to be today, just like Stacey did. By doing this, you lessen the negative influence of your BPD relationship problem areas and broaden your perspective of not only yourself, but your FP relationship as well.

RIPPING THE ROOTS

Below is a list of a dozen possible components that could have added to the probability of you developing BPD and subsequently having an unstable self-image. Place a checkmark next to the possible root to your unstable self-image. Don't focus on how many you check off or how few. It's not the number of roots you identify; it's the process of uncovering them that'll help you understand those early experiences that influenced the creation of your BPD and your unstable self-image.

✓	Unstable Self-Image Roots
	Rejection: I internalized rejection from others as a reflection of my worth or abilities. This reinforced my negative beliefs, making it harder to maintain a stable and positive self-image.
	Inconsistent or negative feedback: I experienced frequent negative feedback or comparisons from parents, teachers, or peers.
	Trauma: I experienced traumatic events that lead to feelings of helplessness, shame, and a distorted sense of self.
	Mental health disorders: Depression, anxiety, and bipolar disorder in myself or my family added to my distorted thinking and emotional instability.
	Social and cultural factors: Societal pressures and social media comparisons amplified my feelings of inadequacy.
	Lack of self-awareness: My lack of self-reflection and awareness made it harder to maintain a consistent self-view.
	Identity issues: My struggles with gender, sexuality, or other cultural issues added to my unstable self-image and significant internal distress.
	Perfectionism: I hold and grew up with unattainable standards that are now associated with shame and dissatisfaction, causing me to feel perpetually "not good enough."
	Peer influence: Peer pressure and the desire to fit in caused me to constantly change who I was to meet others' expectations and added to my variable self-perception.
	Lack of achievement or purpose: My struggles to achieve goals created feelings of failure that led to a lack of sense of purpose and accomplishment and eroded my identity.
	Substance abuse: Substance abuse in my past or present and in my family of origin distorted my self-perception, leaving me feeling uncertain about who I am.
	Relationship issues: My abusive or dysfunctional relationships have severely harmed how I see myself, which amplifies my self-doubt and stability.

Identifying these roots was probably difficult. Many thoughts, feelings, and images may've come up for you. It's what may have kept you from exploring this previously. The next step is to pair the roots you identified with how they impact your relationship problem areas. To do this, try to identify the top three most influential roots that adversely impact your relationship with your FP. Picking just three may be tough, but you can use a separate piece of paper or download more copies at http://www. newharbinger.com/56050. Let's take a look at one of Stacey's responses to provide an example.

1. My childhood trauma of neglect makes me seek validation and fear rejection, straining my relationships because I'm always spying on and don't trust Paul.

Top Three Roots and Relationship Problem Areas

1. _____

_____

2. _____

_____

3. _____

_____

As you uncovered your roots, did you recognize that your sense of self is rooted more in your past rather than in your FP, but it impacts your FP and accentuates your BPD problem areas? Having this insight, you can be more aware of when you're drawn to engage in those maladaptive patterns that contribute to you trying to define yourself through your FP. Knowing who you are, and replacing those BPD maladaptive patterns with self-building stability activities will help you have greater self-awareness and control over those BPD relationship problem areas and destructive beliefs, behaviors, and patterns. Review the list of sense-of-self-stabilizing activities and pick one, or even two, to start with and incorporate them into your daily routine. Don't choose more than two, as you'll get overwhelmed and likely not do any.

SENSE-OF-SELF-STABILIZING ACTIVITIES

- **Self-reflection and journaling:** Spend time regularly reflecting on thoughts, feelings, and actions. Writing helps clarify thinking and uncover patterns in behavior and beliefs.

- **Seek feedback:** Ask for honest feedback from trusted friends, family members, or mentors. They can provide insights into how you are perceived and help identify blind spots.

- **Identify core beliefs:** Reflect on positive core beliefs and values and consider where these beliefs come from and how they influence behavior and decisions. Challenge and reframe those negative or limiting ones.

- **Set personal goals:** Define personal goals and values clearly. Understanding what is important helps align behaviors and decisions with your core values.

- **Practice self-compassion:** Be kind to yourself. Accept that everyone has flaws and makes mistakes. Focus on strengths and achievements rather than shortcomings.

- **Observe and adjust maladaptive patterns:** Pay attention to recurring patterns in behavior, particularly those that are unhelpful or negative. Actively work on changing these patterns by setting small, achievable goals for improvement.

Using the spaces below, list which self-stabilizing activities you're going to incorporate and then identify what time each day and where you'll be to engage in this activity. Doing this links a specific situational cue with a desired response and helps you to automate goal-directed behaviors and improve the likelihood of success.

I am going to do _____ (self-stabilizing activity)

at _____ (time) when I will be _____ (location).

I am going to do _____ (self-stabilizing activity)

at _____ (time) when I will be _____ (location).

You've started your journey of self-discovery to help your relationships grow in healthier directions, increasing your feelings of value and appreciation. Your understanding of yourself will continue to develop as you progress through this workbook. The next section of this chapter will focus on your FP and how your BPD lens influences your perception of them. This lens often leads you to engage in the maladaptive strategy of thought assumptions, causing you to misinterpret neutral facial expressions, tone of voice, and behaviors as negative, rooting your relationship problem areas in your life. Let's unroot them!

Deconstructing the Misperception of My FP

As you've progressed through the first four chapters and the initial section of this one, you've gained valuable insights about yourself and the nature of relationships. Now, we'll focus on how you perceive your FP. This helps you build insight, minimize the adverse influence of BPD and those relationship problem areas, and expand your control over them. We're going to revisit your BPD lens and your FP's facial expressions, tone of voice, and behaviors; but before we do that, let's see how Stacey tends to misperceive her FP, Paul.

Before learning management tools, Stacey's BPD lens made her see Paul's actions in a negative light. When Paul had a serious look with a furrowed brow, her BPD lens drove her to think he was upset or doesn't care about her, causing her to feel rejected. If Paul spoke in a calm voice, her BPD lens interpreted it as him being mad, even when he's just tired. When Paul sat quietly to relax, Stacey's BPD lens made her believe he was pulling away, which made her feel anxious and unloved. Because of her BPD lens, Stacey would assume the worst about Paul, leading to defensive reactions or emotional withdrawal. This misunderstanding created more arguments and made it harder for them to trust each other and stay close.

The next activity is going to help you avoid the BPD lens trap with your FP, just like Stacey, so you can avoid many of the same or similar relationship landmines.

Discovering My FP Without My BPD Lens

The questions below are divided into four categories: self-awareness and perceptions, needs and expectations, communication and conflict resolution, and growth and compatibility. The related relationship problem areas are below each heading title in parentheses, to increase your perspective of each category and the related five questions. These questions ask you to evaluate different aspects of your relationship and your perception of your FP. Circle how authentic, clear-sighted, aware, secure, and genuinely content you feel in your relationship using the rating scale from 0 to 4:

0 = Strongly Disagree

1 = Disagree

2 = Neutral

3 = Agree

4 = Strongly Agree

Self-Awareness and Perception (Frequent Fear of Abandonment, Unpredictable Mood Swings)					
I feel comfortable being my true self around my FP	0	1	2	3	4
I see my FP clearly for who they are	0	1	2	3	4
I don't ignore or distort my FP's behaviors	0	1	2	3	4
I feel secure and respected in this relationship	0	1	2	3	4
I am not afraid of being alone and I genuinely enjoy being with my FP	0	1	2	3	4
Needs and Expectations (Excessive Clinginess or Neediness, Sudden Withdrawal or Silent Treatment, Extreme Jealousy and Control Issues, Testing the Relationship)					
I am clear on my own needs and values in a relationship	0	1	2	3	4
I don't expect my FP to fulfill all my needs	0	1	2	3	4
I communicate my needs effectively to my FP	0	1	2	3	4
I am happy with the level of effort I put into the relationship	0	1	2	3	4
I am open to compromise and finding solutions that work for both of us	0	1	2	3	4
Communication and Conflict Resolution (Overreaction to Perceived Slights, Difficulty in Handling Criticism, Frequent Break-Ups and Make-Ups)					
I listen actively to my FP and I'm not quick to interrupt or judge	0	1	2	3	4
I feel comfortable expressing my feelings and opinions to my FP	0	1	2	3	4
Our arguments don't become overly heated quickly	0	1	2	3	4
We take responsibility for our own actions and words during conflict	0	1	2	3	4
We are able to forgive each other and move on from arguments	0	1	2	3	4

Growth and Compatibility (Difficulty Trusting Positive Experiences)					
My FP encourages me to grow as a person	0	1	2	3	4
We share similar values and life goals	0	1	2	3	4
We have compatible interests and it's ok to enjoy different things	0	1	2	3	4
I feel supported in pursuing my passions and dreams	0	1	2	3	4
There is a sense of fun and shared joy in the relationship	0	1	2	3	4

Now identify those questions that you feel have the greatest impact on the degree to which you feel authentic, clear-sighted, aware, secure, and genuinely content in your relationship. These are likely marked with a 3 or 4. Using the spaces below, explore these results that influenced your perceptions and describe them to help you view your FP more accurately and identify where your BPD relationship problem areas likely add distortion via your BPD lens.

My ratings of self-awareness and perception are attributed to: _____

_____

_____

My ratings of needs and expectations are based on: _____

_____

_____

My ratings of communication and conflict resolution are attributed to: _____

_____

_____

My ratings of growth and compatibility are based on: _____

_____

_____

Seeing yourself and the adverse influence of your relationship problem areas gives you options and inroads to push back against distortion, so you and your FP can be authentic by helping you build a sense of trust and genuine connection. As you continue to grow and control your BPD, you may want to revisit these questions and see how they change over time, just as you'll change over time.

Challenging and Changing My Perceptions

Two parts of BPD often work together to distort how you see your FP and situations: assuming the worst and seeing neutral things as negative. These habits likely started as a way to protect yourself when you were growing up. But now, they're not helping. They're holding you back.

In relationships, these negative perceptions can make you feel on edge. They can damage trust and make things feel unstable. Even small things can feel like big threats, making you react out of fear. This can lead to unhealthy patterns, like pushing people away or acting out, which only brings more stress and confusion.

To make your relationship stronger, you need to notice what's not working and try to fix it. Your BPD might resist this because truth, confidence, and self-awareness take away its power. But you can make your BPD weaker and take back control. Let's start there.

STABILIZING A ONCE UNSTABLE FOUNDATION

The following questions will help you look at your negative thoughts in a new way. They'll encourage you to see your thoughts and feelings from different angles, which can help you figure out if they're just negative assumptions that harm your emotional health and amplify your BPD problem areas or if they're actually helping to build a stronger relationship. This kind of thinking can be tough, so Stacey's answers are included to help guide you. If you run out of space, you can use extra paper if you need to, or you can download a copy of this exercise at http://www.newharbinger.com/56050.

When I feel frustrated or upset, what narratives am I creating about the situation? Are these narratives helping or hindering me, and why might I be using them?

I often think I'm inadequate or unworthy of success. These thoughts reinforce my fear, doubt, and shame from past trauma, and I use them because they feel familiar and protect me from risk and rejection though they hinder my success.

_____

_____

_____

If I could step outside of my own head and observe this scenario objectively, what details might I notice that I'm currently overlooking?

I notice that I'm not giving myself enough credit for my efforts and achievements. I'd likely see that I am overemphasizing my mistakes and underestimating my strengths.

_____

_____

_____

Sometimes past experiences can influence how I perceive the present. Is there a past event that might be coloring my interpretation of this situation?

My history of neglect and emotional abuse has made me doubt my value and capabilities. This past trauma often makes me see present challenges through a lens of fear and inadequacy empowering my BPD.

_____

_____

_____

Instead of focusing solely on what's "wrong," identify any opportunities for growth or learning within this perceived negative situation.

I am working to build resilience, learning to trust myself, and developing healthier relationships. Instead of acting out, I can ask Paul to talk and discuss my fears and doubt.

_____

_____

_____

Imagine a future version of yourself who has mastered managing negativity. What advice would that version give you about navigating this situation?

I would advise myself to acknowledge my progress and to remind myself that setbacks are part of the journey. This version of me would encourage me to believe in my self-worth and to express myself openly, even if it feels uncomfortable.

_____

_____

_____

Recognizing the tendency to skew negatively by making assumptions about various situations and people will help you attain a greater sense of stability. This involves you revisiting this topic when you feel your core content getting activated, empowering your BPD problem areas, so that when that unstable ground starts to rumble, you can catch it before the earthquakes. Seeing your FP more authentically will help you build a foundation of stability in your relationships, which takes us to our final section of this chapter: the distorted perception of your relationship as a whole. Much like building a Lego® tower, let's keep snapping those adaptive strategy bricks on top of one another.

Disentangling My Distorted Relationship

Your internalized fears, like feeling not good enough or unworthy, influence how you see your relationship in unhealthy ways. BPD makes you extra sensitive to things your FP says or does, even if they aren't meant to hurt you. You might see small things as signs they're going to leave you, which can lead to emotional outbursts or pushing them away before they can "hurt" you.

BPD also affects how you see yourself and others, trapping you in patterns that cause pain and make relationships harder. You might stay quiet to avoid conflict, especially if past experiences taught you it wasn't safe to speak up. But that silence can cause more misunderstandings and make you feel even more unsure or alone.

In this chapter, you'll learn how to notice these thoughts and feelings so they don't control you. That way, you can break the cycle and build more stable, healthy relationships. Let's start by going over some simple steps to see your relationship more clearly and reduce the harm from those negative beliefs.

Using Awareness and Openness to Change Bad Habits

The questions below are meant to help you look inside yourself and figure out what might be keeping you from being open in your relationships. It can be tough when your own beliefs work against you, just like they did for Stacey. But by answering these questions, you can start to see things more clearly, understand your place in the relationship, and realize the impact you have on it. Go through the questions to help reduce the negative effects of your BPD relationship problem areas. Included are some common things that can cause distorted thinking. See Stacey's answer to the first question as a helpful example.

What prevents you from expressing your needs?

I'm scared of being rejected or judged and worry that my needs will be a burden to Paul. I've been abandoned before by people I loved, which made this fear even worse. To deal with it, I remind myself that my feelings are important and that Paul cares about me. I try not to keep my fear inside, and instead, I slowly start sharing my needs in small ways to build trust and confidence.

Just like Stacey did, use the questions below to explore and work on your own beliefs and fears about your relationship with your FP. Answer the questions that best fit your situation. If you need more space to write, feel free to use extra paper or download a copy of this exercise at http://www.newharbinger.com/56050.

What prevents you from expressing your needs? This could stem from a fear of rejection or a belief that your needs aren't important.

_____

_____

_____

_____

What drives you to be overly critical of your FP? This might be rooted in internalized beliefs about perfectionism or a fear of intimacy.

_____

_____

_____

_____

What causes you to become defensive during arguments and what do you tend to do? This could be due to a fear of conflict or a belief that you're always wrong.

_____

_____

_____

_____

What prevents you from setting clear boundaries? This might be because you have internalized beliefs about needing to please others or a fear of being alone.

_____

_____

_____

Describe the unhealthy dynamics that added to your past relationships? These experiences might have shaped internalized beliefs about love and what's "normal" in a relationship.

_____

_____

_____

_____

How does your current relationship mimic your past critical or emotionally distant environment? This could have led to internalized beliefs about self-worth and difficulty with intimacy.

_____

_____

_____

Describe how your top three BPD relationship problem areas complicate authentic expression of your wants and needs.

_____

_____

_____

_____

What's a healthier way to let your FP know how your top three relationship struggles are affecting the relationship?

_____

_____

_____

_____

How can you and your FP work together to support each other and openly talk about your top three relationship problem areas?

_____

_____

_____

This process probably wasn't easy, but it helps you see things more clearly and gives you the power to make choices that can improve your relationship. By recognizing your beliefs and fears, you can create a more open and honest connection where you both work on these issues in a healthy way. Keep building patience, support, and self-compassion as you go, so you can celebrate your progress together. When your fears start to distort your view of the relationship, remember to be kind to yourself and use the skills you've learned from this chapter, and the ones you'll keep learning. Also, remember to build your self-worth outside of the relationship, which will help create a stronger, healthier bond.

Setting the Stage for Relationship Success

Using the spaces below, pull together what you learned from this chapter so you can take this information with you and use it in your relationships.

How will the skills you've learned in this chapter help you manage your top three BPD relationship problem areas?

_____

_____

_____

In what ways can the skills you've learned in this chapter help you respond more calmly to disagreements or feedback?

_____

_____

_____

What skills can you apply from this chapter to have greater mood stabilization and maintain consistency in your relationship?

_____

_____

_____

What can you use from this chapter to build a close relationship with your FP?

_____

_____

_____

How can the skills you've learned in this chapter help you increase trust, acceptance, and love in your relationship?

_____

_____

_____

In the next chapter, you'll learn how to deal with your relationship insecurities. You'll look at fears related to attachment and your FP and find ways to break free from anxiety or avoidant behaviors. This chapter will also help you create stronger, more secure relationships by focusing on what you _want_ rather than what you _need_. You'll also work on changing your beliefs, building a positive mindset, and learning how to trust and manage your emotions better in your relationships.

CHAPTER 6

Expose and Evolve from Your Relationship Insecurities

In this chapter, we'll explore the insecurities fueling your BPD and how they affect your relationships. This will help you build healthier attachments and reduce feelings of disappointment, loneliness, and abandonment. You'll learn skills to handle relationship issues and insecurities in healthier ways.

BPD feeds on insecurities, making relationship issues worse. But you can move forward and build stronger, more secure relationships. You might feel tempted to fall back on old habits like clinging or pulling away, and BPD can make you believe you deserve unhealthy relationships by amplifying your insecurities, leading to fights and feelings of rejection and emptiness.

It's time to learn to challenge the fixed mindset BPD creates and develop a growth mindset that embraces openness, care, and love from others. By using the techniques in this chapter, you'll gain better self-control, manage relationship issues more effectively, and build healthier connections with the people who matter most.

Brian will be your guide in this chapter. Let's start by looking at Brian's relationship insecurities and how BPD and his relationship problem areas affected his view of himself and the people around him.

• Brian's Insecure Relationship Tendencies

Brian, 37, lives in Boulder, Colorado, and has always had a hard time with relationships. His friends would say he was either too intense or too distant, and he often felt stuck and frustrated. When he met Lisa, he thought things might finally change. She was kind and understanding, and for a while, their relationship seemed good. But over time, Brian's behavior started to cause problems. His moods would change quickly, one moment he'd be loving and happy, and the next, he'd be angry or upset for reasons that weren't always clear. When he felt hurt or like Lisa didn't understand him, he would pull away completely, giving her the silent treatment or acting like he didn't care.

Brian often tested their relationship in ways that made things harder. He would start arguments for no reason, flirt with other people, or push Lisa away just to see if she would come back. This left Lisa feeling confused and unsure about where she stood. One day, after a big fight, Lisa broke down and told Brian how much his actions were hurting her. Seeing her so upset made Brian realize that his behavior was the real problem, not Lisa. Wanting to fix things, he started therapy, discovered BPD, and learned how to manage his emotions and stop doing things that eroded their relationship. It wasn't easy, but Brian worked hard to change. Over time, he started building a healthier, stronger connection with Lisa, one based on trust and understanding instead of confusion and hurt.

As we go through this chapter, we're going to see how Brian did this, so you can too. To help you do this we've got to get to the root of connection, your attachment pattern, and explore those strategies and choices that strengthen BPD through maladaptive attachment avoidance and anxiety.

Breaking Free from Anxiety and Avoidant Attachment

Imagine having a tug-of-war inside you when it comes to getting close to people. You want to be close, but at the same time, you feel scared and want to pull away. This push-and-pull can be really confusing, especially when you don't even notice it happening. It's like your brain is on autopilot, trying to protect you from feeling hurt or rejected. Everyone with BPD feels this differently, but it's often tied to how you attach to others.

Sometimes, this struggle comes from anxious or avoidant attachment styles. It can feel like you're always on edge, like you're in danger even when you're not. This can cause you to react in ways that push people away, making relationships harder. To change this, you need to learn new ways to handle these feelings instead of letting BPD control you.

Because those BPD thoughts, feelings, and memories make you extra sensitive to abandonment, rejection, and emptiness, you feel drawn to your FP for comfort and safety. When they're there for you, you feel better and can manage your emotions. When your FP seems distant or unavailable, you feel overwhelmed by hurt, anger, fear, or sadness. This insecurity can lead to attachment anxiety, where you worry about being abandoned or rejected. You might also try to protect yourself by pushing people away or acting like you don't need them; this is called attachment avoidance. Both reactions entail your BPD trying to convince you that you're unimportant or invisible because your FP isn't there, even though that's not true. That BPD lens keeps working until you break free.

Let's work on moving your thoughts and behaviors away from anxiety and avoidance, and toward more secure and healthy strategies.

My Pathway to a More Secure Attachment

This exercise will help you understand how you feel and act in relationships based upon your attachment patterns. By thinking about your worries and rating how much they affect you, you'll be able to identify if you tend to feel insecure, avoid close relationships, or get anxious easily. This insight will help you see what makes you feel nervous or unsure with your FP and will help you find ways to feel better and more secure in your relationships.

To start this exercise, first identify your perceived threat about your FP from the list or write your own if it's not there.

☐ Fear of them being away for a long time

☐ Intense worry about not being understood or heard by them

☐ Fear of them not being emotionally available when you need them

☐ Sense of dread about being rejected or abandoned

☐ Other: _____

Next, mark those statements that fit for you about how you feel and act in relationships; these are grouped into "avoidant" and "anxious attachment." You'll then rate how many you marked within each section to derive a total score.

Anxious attachment and safety:

☐ I feel unsafe or insecure in my relationships, even when there is no apparent danger.

☐ I often doubt the stability of my relationships without any clear reason.

☐ I experience physical anxiety symptoms like trembling, sweating, or a quickened heart rate in response to relationship stress.

☐ I have difficulty setting boundaries or saying no in my relationships.

☐ I feel overwhelmed by anxiety or fear when I think about the possibility of relationship conflicts.

☐ I frequently question whether my FP truly cares about me, even without evidence to support my doubts.

☐ I find myself constantly seeking reassurance from my FP to feel secure.

_____ **Total Score**

Anxious attachment and intimacy:

☐ I have a strong desire to be close to others but often feel insecure about the relationship.

☐ I feel highly distressed by misunderstandings or conflicts in my relationships.

☐ I tend to jump to negative conclusions about my FP's intentions without rationally assessing the situation.

☐ I experience jealousy toward my FP's other relationships and friendships.

☐ I engage in manipulative behaviors to seek reassurance from my FP.

☐ I withdraw or threaten to withdraw when conflicts arise in my relationship.

☐ I pursue, nag, or criticize my FP in an effort to get them to change.

_____ **Total Score**

Avoidant attachment and independence:

☐ I value self-sufficiency and independence to the point where it can interfere with intimacy.

☐ I feel uncomfortable sharing deep feelings with others.

☐ I tend to avoid or delay commitment in my relationships.

☐ I focus on my FP's flaws more than their positive qualities.

☐ I feel anxious or controlled when my FP seeks closeness or intimacy.

☐ I exhibit distancing behaviors, such as withdrawing or pulling back from intimate situations.

☐ I fear becoming too needy or dependent on my FP.

_____ **Total Score**

Put your total scores for each insecure attachment category below.

Anxious Attachment and Safety	Anxious Attachment and Intimacy	Avoidant Attachment and Independence

We'll be applying this information after the next exercise. For now, let's focus on behaviors that help promote secure attachment. Using the same method you used earlier, identify the statements that fit for you and describe strategies you think would work best for building a safe and healthy relationship. As you're marking your answers below, don't get caught up in which is "better." This isn't about better; it's about finding what fits best for you.

Building Secure Attachment:

Reflect, communicate, reinforce positivity:

☐ I can regularly practice self-reflection to identify and address any sources of doubt.

☐ I will communicate openly about my feelings and concerns.

☐ I am able to reinforce positive affirmations and self-worth regularly for me and my FP.

_____ **Total Score**

Share, connect, overcome barriers:

☐ I will practice sharing my thoughts and feelings regularly.

☐ I can engage in activities that foster emotional closeness, such as deep conversations or shared hobbies.

☐ I will work on identifying and addressing my fears and barriers to intimacy.

_____ **Total Score**

Listen, be calm, express clearly:

☐ I can develop active listening skills to fully understand my FP's perspective.

☐ I am able to take a moment to breathe and calm down before responding to conflicts.

☐ I will use "I" statements to express how I feel without placing blame.

_____ **Total Score**

Appreciate, empathize, prioritize growth:

☐ I am able to make a list of qualities I appreciate in my FP and review it regularly.

☐ I will practice empathy by putting myself in my FP's shoes.

☐ I can focus on the bigger picture and the overall health of the relationship rather than dwelling on minor flaws.

_____ **Total Score**

Accountability, forgiveness, collaborative solutions:

☐ I will practice taking responsibility for my actions and offering genuine apologies when necessary.

☐ I can work on letting go of grudges and moving forward after resolving conflicts.

☐ I am able to collaborate with my FP to find mutually beneficial solutions to problems.

_____ **Total Score**

Confidence, self-assurance, independence:

☐ I can build my self-esteem through activities and achievements that boost my confidence.

☐ I will practice self-assurance techniques, such as positive self-talk and mindfulness.

☐ I am able to establish and maintain personal boundaries and interests outside of the relationship.

_____ **Total Score**

Balance, goals, open communication:

☐ I am able to spend quality time with my FP as well as time pursuing my own interests and friendships.

☐ I can set personal goals and work toward them independently of my relationship.

☐ I will communicate openly about my need for both closeness and independence and respect their needs as well.

_____ **Total Score**

Put your total scores for each secure attachment behavior category below.

Reflect, Communicate, Reinforce Positivity	Share, Connect, Overcome Barriers	Listen, Be Calm, Express Clearly
Appreciate, Empathize, Prioritize Growth	Accountability, Forgiveness, Collaborative Solutions	Confidence, Self-Assurance, Independence
Balance, Goals, Open Communication		

List your highest rated insecure attachment category: _____

List your two highest rated secure attachment categories: _____

_____

You can now see which insecure attachment type is affecting you the most, and it's likely made worse by your BPD and your relationship problem areas. But there's good news—you've also found your top two secure attachment areas. These will help you move from feeling stuck in your insecurity to feeling more free and secure in your relationships. I've added two general secure attachment behavioral approaches for you to use to implement your highest-rated secure attachment categories. Work to augment them to fit your interpersonal style, implement them slowly, and allow them to become healthy habits over time.

1. **Practice open communication:** Talk honestly about your feelings, needs, and concerns with your FP. Let them know what's on your mind and be willing to listen to their thoughts too. This helps build trust and makes both of you feel more connected and understood.

2. **Focus on building trust**: Show that you can be dependable by keeping your promises and being consistent in your actions. At the same time, give the other person room to be themselves and respect their boundaries. Trust grows when both people feel safe and respected.

Building Security

Next, you're going to take one of your identified insecure thoughts or behaviors from one of your highest-rated insecure categories, like *I feel really anxious or scared when I think about arguments in my relationship*. Now pair it with one of your identified secure thoughts or behaviors from one of your highest-rated secure categories, like *I can practice listening carefully so I can better understand what my FP is feeling*. Doing this helps you replace insecure attachment patterns with secure ones. You can use extra paper if you need to, or you can download a copy of this exercise at http://www.newharbinger.com/56050.

Here's an example of one of Brian's answers to help:

Instead of (Insecure Thought/Behavior): Constantly needing reassurance from my FP when I sense a threat to my attachment, I'm going to (Secure Thought/Behavior): practice self-assurance techniques like positive self-talk and mindfulness to cultivate inner security.

Instead of (Insecure Thought/Behavior): _____

_____

when I sense a threat to my attachment, I'm going to (Secure Thought/Behavior): _____

_____

Instead of (Insecure Thought/Behavior):_____

_____

when I sense a threat to my attachment, I'm going to (Secure Thought/Behavior): _____

_____

You're on the path to overcoming insecure attachment and the thoughts and behaviors that've kept your relationship problem areas ever-present. Using the information above, describe how moving from an insecure to a more secure thought/behavior approach helps lessen the adverse influence of your top three BPD relationship problem areas. You can use extra paper if you need to, or you can download a copy of this exercise at http://www.newharbinger.com/56050.

One of Brian's responses is included below to help you. Remember, one of his problem areas was *testing the relationship.*

Describe how shifting from an insecure thought or behavior to a more secure one helps you reduce the negative impact of your BPD relationship problem areas.

When I stopped testing Lisa and took responsibility for my actions, apologizing when needed, it helped rebuild trust and showed me I don't need to test her love to feel secure.

Describe how shifting from an insecure thought or behavior to a more secure one helps you reduce the negative impact of your BPD relationship problem areas.

_____

_____

_____

_____

Describe how shifting from an insecure thought or behavior to a more secure one helps you reduce the negative impact of your BPD relationship problem areas.

_____

_____

_____

_____

You're building insight and understanding into your central issues and concerns that have been perpetuated by BPD, while also recognizing that a healthy relationship is about both people feeling valued and appreciated. With what you've learned so far, we'll now focus on practical steps to make these insights stronger to help create the relationship you truly want, not just what you feel you dependently need.

The Relationship You Want, Not Need

Finding comfort in chaos often comes from your past, where instability felt normal because you grew up in a tough environment. Even if chaos feels familiar, it's not healthy. Feeling safe in unstable situations but anxious when things are calm creates a harmful pattern. Over time, this comfort in chaos became part of your insecure attachment, fueling your BPD and trapping you in need-based relationships. These relationships gave you a false sense of safety, making you feel secure only when there was chaos. Now, it's time to break free from that cycle.

To start, you need to understand the difference between need-based and want-based relationships. A "need-based" relationship is when you're with someone because you feel you can't be okay without them. It feels like you need the relationship to exist, to be seen, or even to breathe. This creates constant worry, fear, or even feeling trapped. It's more about needing them in order to feel whole than genuinely wanting to be with them.

A "want-based" relationship is different. It's when you're with someone because you enjoy their company, not because you depend on them. It's built on respect, shared interests, and open communication. In these relationships, you feel safe and secure because you're together by choice, not because of unhealthy need.

Need-based and want-based relationships are two ends of a spectrum. Healthy relationships are built on choice and mutual enjoyment, not fear or dependency. In healthy connections, you feel free to be yourself and make mistakes. When need takes over, you feel pressured to be perfect, thinking, *I better not mess this up or they'll leave me.* The goal is to shift from dependency to genuine, secure connections.

Look at your past relationships. BPD may have kept you stuck in need-based connections. If "want-based" relationships feel unfamiliar, it shows how much BPD has shaped your experiences. But that can change. Now is the time to dig deep, understand your true feelings, and build the relationships you truly want.

Rebuilding Secure Relationships from Chaotic Roots

This exercise is going to guide you through the exploration of how your early experiences of chaos shaped your attachment styles and relationship problem areas and needs. We'll work on transforming these patterns to build connections based on "want" rather than "need." Building healthy relationships takes time and work, so be patient with yourself and celebrate every little step you take forward. If you find yourself struggling with negative patterns or unhealthy neediness, take a break and then return to the exercise when you're ready.

Before you begin the exercise, reflect on your past and present feelings about relationships. This exercise is designed to help you uncover patterns, understand your emotional responses, and identify healthy strategies for building fulfilling connections. Approach each prompt with honesty and an open mind, allowing yourself the space to explore your thoughts and emotions more closely.

Describe a childhood experience that felt chaotic or unpredictable and how this environment makes you feel today looking back on it (e.g., anxious, unsafe, insecure).

_____

_____

_____

Explain how the fear of being alone (in a chaotic environment) manifests into a feeling of needing anyone or someone in your life, regardless of their behavior.

_____

_____

_____

Identify past instances where you felt a strong "need" for someone in your life, even if the relationship wasn't healthy and what emotions fueled this need (e.g., fear of abandonment, loneliness, a belief you weren't "enough").

_____

_____

_____

How did this "need" lead to creation or perpetuation of your relationship problem areas (e.g., tolerating disrespect, neglecting your own needs, making excuses for bad behavior)?

_____

_____

_____

Considering what you've learned so far, what self-statements can you use to push back the internal belief that you are "not enough" and unworthy of love?

_____

_____

_____

Push aside your top three relationship problem areas and identify healthy qualities you want in a relationship (e.g., emotional support, respectful communication, shared values).

_____

_____

_____

How can you encourage your FP to develop the qualities you want to improve your relationship issues (e.g., demonstrate the qualities, talk about them openly, praise your FP when they show these qualities)?

_____

_____

_____

You've uncovered a lot of insightful information that will help you understand your past and feelings, build better habits, and work toward healthier, happier connections with your FP. For the next step, review the adaptive strategies listed below to help you identify and develop qualities within yourself, so you can feel more fulfilled, secure, and ready for a healthy relationship based on "want" rather than "need." Then, answer the insight-building questions and activity to further strengthen what you've learned. Choose no more than three strategies to focus on and turn into lasting habits to prevent overwhelm.

☐ **Build self-empathy:** Try to understand your own feelings and see things from someone else's point of view.

☐ **Set healthy boundaries:** Sometimes saying no or avoiding bad habits helps you be more supportive when you can say yes to yourself and others.

☐ **Practice self-compassion:** Be kind to yourself when you make mistakes and try not to take it out on others.

☐ **Focus on your strengths:** Notice what you're good at and be proud of it. Don't downplay your abilities.

☐ **Invest in personal growth:** Keep learning new things and growing, both on your own and with others.

☐ **Identify your own needs and wants:** Remember to do healthy things that make you happy and feel good.

How can you use the strategies you've identified to make your life more stable and predictable (like setting routines, taking care of yourself, and using healthy ways to cope)?

_____

_____

_____

_____

Imagine yourself setting boundaries and clearly stating your needs in your relationship. How would that feel (like feeling strong, confident, safe, or secure)?

_____

_____

_____

Look over your answers and explain how this new way of thinking changes how you build and maintain positive relationship habits.

_____

_____

_____

Finally, picture yourself in a relationship where you focus on the positive qualities you've chosen. Try to draw this image, even if you're not great at drawing. Just express what you see in your mind. The goal is to create a picture that shows the kind of relationship you *want*, not one you *need*.

Moving from your anxious and avoidant attachment behaviors and patterns to your relationship wants is an important step in your growth. Now, let's focus on your beliefs. We've mentioned them before, but it's time to dive deeper into your beliefs about yourself and your FP to lessen the negative impact of your BPD and your relationship problem areas.

Reshaping Your Beliefs

Now, we're going to work on changing the way you think to help build healthy relationships, trust your FP more, and have better self-control. This means strengthening positive beliefs about yourself to help uncover and get rid of fears and insecurities driven by BPD.

Your Empowering Mindset

The way you talk to yourself shapes how you see the world. Changing negative thoughts can build a healthier mindset. For example, instead of thinking, *If my FP doesn't text back right away, they don't care,* try, *They might be busy, it doesn't mean they don't care.* Shifting your thoughts this way helps you feel more secure and calm, reducing BPD triggers and improving your relationship. This simple change can greatly impact how you feel about yourself, your relationship, and how you interact with your FP.

To do this, you need to develop a healthier mindset about yourself, others, your FP, and your world. Recognizing and mastering your mindset helps reduce negative thoughts and BPD patterns while increasing the chances of positive outcomes in your relationship. It's about how you view yourself, your FP, and your relationship's future. Your feelings about closeness, self-worth, and desires all influence your expectations. Your mindset is crucial to this change. Let's explore two types of mindsets: growth and fixed.

Fixed Mindset	Growth Mindset
A fixed mindset is when you believe your abilities and intelligence can't change. People with this mindset think they're born a certain way and can't get better at things.	A growth mindset is when you believe you can get better at things through hard work and practice. People with this mindset see challenges as chances to learn and grow.

When you look at these two types of mindsets side by side, you can see which one BPD feeds off of to keep you stuck. If your mindset is fixated on thoughts like being abandoned, rejected, feeling empty, failing, or being alone, you end up feeling trapped in a pit of sadness. But the opposite, the growth mindset, helps you to grow and try out new strategies and ways of thinking that can change your life for the better. It helps you make changes that you can learn and grow from and build a relationship where you can thrive.

The chart below will help you learn more about the difference between a fixed mindset and a growth mindset as they relate to different beliefs and behaviors. Review these and then we'll use this knowledge to help you incorporate them into your life to help you make positive changes.

Aspect	Fixed Mindset	Growth Mindset
Belief in change	My abilities are static	My abilities can be developed
Approach to challenges	I avoid challenges	I embrace challenges
Response to feedback	I get defensive, see feedback as criticism	I'm open to feedback. I see it as helpful
Effort and persistence	I see my effort as fruitless	I see that my effort leads to mastery and improvement
View on failure	My failure, any perceived failure, defines me and my abilities	My failure is a learning opportunity
Reaction to others' success	I feel threatened by others' success	I feel inspired and motivated by others' success
Risk-taking	I avoid risks to prevent failure	I take suitable risks knowing they are part of the learning process

In the exercise below, you're going to be asked to write a letter to your BPD, explaining that you see how it tricks you into sticking with a fixed mindset. Then, you'll write a letter to yourself about how you're going to recognize and adopt a growth mindset in your life and relationships. I've included Brian's letters as examples to guide you.

To my BPD,

I see how you try to trick me into thinking I can't change or get better, making me believe my skills are stuck and won't improve. You make me avoid challenges, get upset when people give me advice, and feel like any mistake means I'm a failure. You make me feel bad when others do well and scared to take risks that could help me grow. But now, I know what you're doing, and I'm ready to fight back. I believe I can grow, learn, and do great things beyond what you say. You're losing your grip on me, and I'm going to use a growth mindset to take back my life.

Dear Brian,

I am committed to using a growth mindset in my life and relationships. I believe I can get better at things, and I will face challenges with a positive attitude. I'll be open to feedback and see it as a way to help me grow. I know that working hard helps me improve, and I will see failures as chances to learn. I'll be inspired by other people's success and take smart risks because I know they help me learn. With this mindset, I'm ready to grow and do my best in all parts of my life.

You can see the big difference between the two letters, which shows how these mindsets can affect you. Now that you've read Brian's letters, write your own in your journal or on a piece of paper. Look at them from time to time or even rewrite them as you keep working on your growth mindset. You can also download a copy of this exercise at http://www.newharbinger.com/56050.

To my BPD,

_____

_____

_____

_____

_____

_____

Dear _____ (your name),

_____

_____

_____

_____

_____

_____

As you read through your letters, focus on the way you spoke to yourself and see things affecting your mindset. Remember, your mindset is shaped by all those things you tell yourself. These thoughts can help you adopt a growth mindset that encourages you to move beyond your BPD and relationship problem areas.

STRENGTHENING YOUR RELATIONSHIP GROWTH MINDSET

Adopting a growth mindset can truly improve your life and relationships, but it's not easy. It's like pulling weeds from a garden: you work to get rid of them but more always seem to come back, causing you to have to continually pull weeds. After a while you may want to just give up and let those weeds win, but we're not going to do that! The fixed mindset thoughts and behaviors (weeds) that are holding you back manifest as *I never get anything right in relationships*, and these can make you feel bad and lead to actions that cause you to give in to BPD, to push others away, or default to those relationship problem areas, such as testing your FP or having difficulty trusting positive experiences. But, if you can catch and pull these negative thoughts, feelings, and behaviors and replace them with positive ones, like weeds with flowers, you'll start to notice that you feel empowered to overcome challenges and build stronger, healthier relationships.

Before you start the exercise, take a look at Brian's answer to identify his fixed mindset relationship thought and behavior amplifiers and how they influence his BPD relationship problem areas.

I struggle with mood swings, shutting down when I'm hurt, and testing Lisa's commitment by starting fights or pushing her away. My fear of losing her makes me jealous and clingy, leading to constant arguments. Deep down, I feel like I can't change, and when she leaves, it feels like proof I'll always lose the people I care about.

Now it's your turn. Write yours below and be as open as you can and consider your top three BPD relationship problem areas and how they influence a fixed mindset.

Identify your fixed mindset relationship thought and behavior amplifiers and how they influence your BPD relationship problem areas

_____

_____

_____

_____

_____

Before you flip those fixed mindset relationship thought and behavior amplifiers into growth-oriented positive ones, let's look at Brian's.

I sometimes get scared Lisa will leave me, and that fear makes me want to act in ways that could hurt our relationship. But I've learned to remind myself that she's with me because she cares. When I start to overreact, I stop and think about the good times we've had and how every couple faces challenges, it doesn't mean she'll leave. Instead of letting my feelings take over, I focus on calmly sharing what's on my mind. Even after small arguments, I remind myself that the positive moments we've built don't just disappear. By trusting in our connection and working on my reactions, I feel more confident in our relationship and happier overall.

Brian put his skills to work, and now it's your turn. Before starting, think about how your positive thoughts and actions can help you grow and improve your relationship. For this exercise, start by writing your fear-based or unhealthy thoughts and behaviors in the first column. Then, in the second column, write down positive and growth-focused alternatives for each one. Next, describe how these new thoughts and behaviors could make a difference in your actions and your relationship. Finally, use your answers to create a few key ideas or actions that show a growth mindset you can use to build stronger, healthier relationships.

For this exercise, consider three things:

1. What do you admire about your favorite person, like their kindness or patience, and how often can you show appreciation?

2. How can you use disagreements as a chance to learn and grow together, handling things better next time?

3. How can you and your FP support each other's goals by encouraging and believing in each other? Now, let's put these ideas into action by writing down a positive, growth-focused thought or behavior for each fear-based one as you begin the exercise.

Maladaptive and fear-based	Positive, adaptive, and growth-encouraging

Describe the impact these positive, adaptive, and growth-encouraging thoughts and behaviors have on your actions and relationship problem areas.

_____

_____

_____

_____

Use your previous responses to write out your growth mindset relationship thoughts and behaviors that you can practice daily to strengthen your relationships.

_____

_____

_____

_____

Remember, changing how you think takes time and effort. By shifting away from your BPD relationship maladaptive beliefs, behaviors, and patterns, you'll start to build healthier and more rewarding relationships. Now, let's take the next step and focus on building trust and mastering your emotions, as this will strengthen the foundation of your relationship and help you create a deeper connection.

Secure Your Relationship Through Trust and Self-Mastery

Building a healthy relationship goes beyond trust and self-control. It's about overcoming insecurities, creating secure attachment, and wanting the relationship, not needing it. This chapter has taught you how to manage insecure attachment and work toward relationships you truly want.

Insecure attachment and feeling incomplete without a relationship can damage trust and cause misunderstandings, creating a harmful cycle. To break this, build self-confidence and address insecurities rooted in your past, not your current relationship. Talking openly with your FP about your fears can weaken BPD-driven insecurities. A supportive FP will listen and help you feel valued, but it's crucial not to let BPD create new barriers. Now, it's time to use what you've learned to strengthen self-control and reduce insecurities that harm your relationship.

Overcoming Mistrust and Improving Your Self-Control in Relationships

This exercise will help you deal with trust issues and self-control challenges in your relationships. You'll look back at past situations, and it might bring up some tough feelings, but that's okay. Remember the strategies you've learned and use them as you think about these situations, without blaming or putting yourself down. Try to resist BPD's influence and focus on being your true self.

Think about and describe three times you've felt mistrust in your relationship and what caused you to feel this way, and whether it is linked to your past and your relationship problem areas. Example: "I feel uneasy when my FP gets messages from unknown contacts."

1. _____

_____

_____

2. _____

_____

_____

3. _____

_____

_____

What are your go-to feelings of mistrust (e.g., jealousy, anger, fear)? Can you share these with your FP, and what would help you talk about them openly?

_____

_____

_____

Create a plan, alone or with your FP, to address these feelings. What steps can build trust and ease your concerns?

_____

_____

_____

_____

What situations cause you to lose control, and why do these situations trigger you? Are they linked to unresolved issues or insecurities? Example: "I lose control when arguments get heated."

_____

_____

_____

What can you do to stay in control and calm during these moments? Think of strategies like taking a timeout or using deep breathing.

_____

_____

_____

What can you and your FP do together to build trust and openness, like sharing daily highlights or having heart-to-heart talks? List some activities where you felt connected and open, or consider what you both enjoy.

_____

_____

_____

What can each of you do to help maintain self-control, like using a code word during disagreements or agreeing on a cooling-off period?

_____

_____

_____

List three ways to positively reinforce trust and self-control, like praising honesty or staying calm during conflicts.

1. _____

2. _____

3. _____

Pick two days each week to focus on reinforcing trust and self-control and track any positive changes in your relationship using your calendar or a sheet of paper.

You've made a big step in dealing with relationship mistrust and building self-control. Thinking about past situations can be hard and bring up a lot of emotions, but you've been brave in facing them. Remember, it's about progress, not perfection. Use the strategies you've learned without blaming yourself. You've stayed true to yourself and resisted BPD's influence on your relationship problem areas, which is a huge achievement.

Setting the Stage for Relationship Success

Using the spaces below, pull together what you learned from this chapter so you can take this information with you and use it in your relationships.

How will the skills you've learned in this chapter help you manage your top three BPD relationship problem areas?

_____

_____

_____

_____

In what ways can the skills you've learned in this chapter help you respond more calmly to disagreements or feedback?

_____

_____

_____

_____

What skills can you apply from this chapter to have greater mood stabilization and maintain consistency in your relationship?

_____

_____

_____

_____

What can you use from this chapter to build a close relationship with your FP?

_____

_____

_____

_____

How can the skills you've learned in this chapter help you increase trust, acceptance, and love in your relationship?

_____

_____

_____

_____

Now that you've learned skills to help you recognize and overcome relationship insecurities, it's time to move forward and explore how you can thrive in relationships, even while managing BPD relationship problem areas. In chapter 7, we'll dive deeper into intimacy, how to embrace your true self, and how to improve communication in a way that builds stronger, more loving connections. You've already started laying the groundwork for secure, healthy relationships, now let's take it a step further by focusing on authenticity and overcoming common challenges, like communication breakdowns.

CHAPTER 7

Thriving and Overcoming BPD Intimacy Challenges

Intimacy is about forming close and loving bonds with others, which can be really tough when you have BPD. In this chapter, you'll learn how to understand and improve the important parts of your relationship with your FP. Being in a relationship when you have BPD can sometimes feel like there's a big wall between you and your FP. It's hard to explain, making it tricky to ask for more honesty, care, and love from them. You might really want these things, but fear can get in the way, causing you to feel desperate. This desperation can trigger your BPD beliefs, behaviors, and patterns which can actually make your relationship problems worse and make it harder for you to get what you need from the relationship.

This chapter will help you take another step toward meeting your relationship needs and lessening the negative effects of BPD. It'll show you how to feel closer to your FP, be yourself, and let your true self shine. Before we begin, let's take a look at Paula and Leon and the challenges they face with intimacy.

• Paula and Leon's Struggles of Intimacy

Paula and Leon had always been close, but lately, things had changed. Paula, who struggles with frequent fear of abandonment, started pulling away from Leon, even though she cared deeply about him. She was scared he would leave her, so she put up walls, hid her feelings, and pretended everything was fine. However, this only made her feel more isolated and disconnected. Leon could sense something was wrong but didn't know how to help. He wanted them to talk openly, but whenever he tried to get close, Paula overreacted due to her difficulty trusting positive experiences. Instead of accepting his support, she would shut down or lash out, which only made matters worse, and it was hard for her to see that she often overreacted to perceived slights. This made it feel like there was a barrier between them, one that Leon felt he couldn't break through.

Paula hated acting this way but didn't know how to stop. Her fear of abandonment led her to keep Leon at a distance, thinking it would protect her from getting hurt, but it only made things worse, as she felt hurt and alone often even when Leon was close. She felt like she was losing herself and letting her BPD control her actions, especially when she would suddenly withdraw or give him the silent treatment. Both Paula and Leon were stuck in a painful cycle. Paula's fear of abandonment drove her to act in ways that weren't true to herself, while Leon's frustration also deepened the distance between them. They both wanted to connect but didn't know how to overcome the BPD relationship problem areas that were pulling them apart.

Paula and Leon's story might sound familiar to your struggles with your FP. Just like they did, you'll learn to understand and embrace the real you while working toward a healthier, happier relationship.

Authenticity, Appreciation, and Love

Intimacy is about opening up to others, especially your FP, and showing your true self. While people often think of intimacy as physical, it goes much deeper. It includes emotional, intellectual, spiritual, and social bonds. These connections shape how close you feel to your FP, family, friends, or coworkers. The more genuine you can be, the deeper and more fulfilling your relationships become.

BPD makes being your true self feel like an uphill battle, amplifying relationship issues. But intimacy isn't all-or-nothing. Every relationship has its own level and type of closeness. By appreciating yourself, recognizing your worth, and allowing yourself to be loved despite BPD's challenges, you can build deeper, more meaningful connections. The exercise below will help you gain insight and see the true value of being you.

The True You

Find a quiet, relaxing place where you can focus without any distractions. Take your time with each part of the following exercise, there's no need to rush. Think deeply and be as honest and open with yourself as you can. Some parts might seem harder than others, and that's totally okay. If things get tough or confusing, don't be too hard on yourself. Now, let's begin by looking closely at the version of yourself that might not be the real you (your false self) then explore your true self (the authentic you). You'll then learn how to see your genuine self and turn that into action to help you move closer to your FP.

UNCOVERING YOUR FALSE SELF

List some situations where you felt like you had to wear a "mask."

_____

_____

_____

_____

_____

What emotions or fears led you to act in a way that wasn't authentic?

_____

_____

_____

How did these behaviors affect your relationship problem areas?

_____

_____

_____

RECOGNIZING YOUR AUTHENTIC SELF

Describe who you are when you're alone, without the influence or expectations of others.

_____

_____

_____

_____

List your true values and beliefs, regardless of what others might think.

_____

_____

_____

_____

Which of the following strategies can you use to express yourself authentically when you feel safe and secure?

☐ Speak openly and honestly about my thoughts and feelings.

☐ Express my needs and boundaries clearly.

☐ Show vulnerability by admitting when I'm unsure or need help.

☐ Engage in activities or hobbies that genuinely interest me.

☐ Display my emotions openly, whether it's joy, sadness, or excitement.

Describe how you'll use these strategies to be your more authentic self.

_____

_____

_____

_____

NURTURING LOVE FOR YOURSELF

Think of a recent situation where you felt hurt or disappointed in yourself.

_____

_____

_____

Describe how you would comfort a close friend in the same situation. What would you say to them?

_____

_____

_____

_____

_____

Now, rewrite those words saying them to yourself, and describe how it feels to give yourself that same kindness.

_____

_____

_____

_____

_____

LOVING ACTIONS TOWARD YOUR FP

Describe how you can show love and appreciation to your FP without losing your authenticity. Included are five suggestions to help, but feel free to use your own too.

- ☐ Share your feelings and fears and be emotionally vulnerable to create a strong bond of trust and intimacy.

- ☐ Collaborate on future aspirations sharing your dreams and goals to foster a sense of unity.

- ☐ Engage in acts of kindness or affection to keep things fun in your relationship and show you care.

- ☐ Get closer with your FP through touch, not just quick hugs. Think about how you both like to be touched to feel safe and connected.

- ☐ Be their rock through thick and thin, offer unwavering belief in them.

I can show my love and appreciation by _____

_____

_____

List some loving actions you can take that respect both your needs and those of your FP.

_____

_____

_____

Describe how loving yourself changes the way you love your FP. Included are five suggestions to help you, but feel free to use your own as well.

- ☐ When I feel good about myself, I have clearer expectations and know my limits.

- ☐ Being open and honest with my FP helps us connect on a deeper level.

- ☐ Feeling secure in myself prevents me from becoming too dependent on my FP.

- ☐ Understanding my own emotions makes it easier to understand how my FP feels.

- ☐ Being true to myself helps me build a genuine and honest relationship with my FP.

Explain what actions you'll take here.

_____

_____

_____

How does self-discovery and self-love help reduce BPD relationship issues and improve authenticity with your FP?

_____

_____

_____

Now that you've finished this exercise, take a moment to review your answers. Think about what you've learned and how you can use it in your daily life. It's good to check back on your progress from time to time. This exercise is here to help you on your journey of self-discovery, showing your true worth and helping you build self-appreciation and love, even while dealing with BPD. By growing your authentic self, you can share yourself with your FP in a healthier way.

One big way to feel safer and show your true self is through communication. You learned these earlier in the workbook, but let's review them and pair them with what you've learned recently. Before we do that, let's look at how Paula and Leon used these skills, like the sandwich method which you'll learn in a moment, to avoid communication problems.

• The Art of Our Connection

Paula and Leon have been working to improve their relationship by trying new communication methods. Paula used to bring up issues immediately due to BPD-driven anxiety and fear, which often led to arguments. She worried Leon didn't care or might leave her, especially when he was busy. Now, she's learning to wait for better times to talk, which has made things calmer and eased her fear of abandonment.

When Paula felt ignored because Leon was working long hours, she used the "sandwich" method: starting with appreciation, gently sharing her concerns, and ending with reassurance. This helped Leon feel understood and made Paula trust his positive reactions more, which she used to struggle with.

Leon has improved too, clearly stating his needs, like asking for quiet time after work, preventing small problems from growing. These changes have helped Paula manage her fear of abandonment, trust good moments, and avoid overreacting, making their relationship feel closer and more loving.

Now it's time to learn the tips and skills that Paula and Leon used to strengthen their relationship and stop BPD from causing fights and communication problems.

Avoiding Communication Breakdown

BPD can make conversations intense, turning small things into a big deal and making you worry that your FP will leave. This fear of abandonment and rejection drives you to react strongly and think in extremes, where everything feels all good or all bad, a.k.a. splitting. This makes it harder to find middle ground and can lead to misunderstandings. When your emotions take over, you might say things in the moment that you later regret, turning a small issue into a bigger fight, and making your

BPD relationship problems worse. The strategies you're about to learn will help your true self get your needs and feelings across to your FP in a healthier way.

Whenever Paula tried to talk to Leon about something personal, her BPD would kick in, putting her on the defensive. Even though she was working on being her true self and building love, she was missing key communication skills. You're going to learn those skills now, so you can feel more empowered, just like Paula did, and making your sandwich is a big part of it.

THE SANDWICH TECHNIQUE

One of the techniques that really helped Paula with her communication was the sandwich technique. Let's check out how Paula used it to help her.

Paula had been feeling distant from Leon and wanted to address it without causing a fight. She realized the issue was their lack of quality time, which made her feel anxious and disconnected.

When they sat down to talk, Paula began with, "I really appreciate how supportive you've been lately. It means a lot to me." This made Leon feel valued and set a positive tone. Then, she gently shared her concern, saying, "I've been feeling disconnected when we don't spend as much time together. It's important to me that we reconnect more often." She focused on her feelings and needs without blaming Leon.

To end on a positive note, Paula added, "I know we can work through this because we've always been good at solving things together." This reassured Leon of her commitment. By using this approach, Paula had a calm, productive conversation that left them both feeling more connected and understood.

Now it's your turn to gather your "sandwich" ingredients and put them together. I've added some helpful tips to guide you. This might be a new way of expressing your needs, so be patient with yourself and try not to let BPD drag you back into old relationship problems. Learning new skills takes time and patience.

HELPFUL SANDWICH INGREDIENTS

Something you appreciate about your FP	The tense or possible emotionally-activating issue	Another positive statement, showing you're committed to making things work
"I appreciate how you always listen when I need to talk."	"I've been feeling a bit distant and think spending more quality time together would help."	"I believe we can get through this because we've always been a strong team."

Something you appreciate about your FP	The tense or possible emotionally-activating issue	Another positive statement, showing you're committed to making things work
"I'm grateful for your support, no matter what."	"I get overwhelmed when we argue, and I think it would be better if we talked more calmly."	"I'm committed to working things out together, like we've done before."
"I love that we can still laugh, even in hard times."	"I feel stressed when plans change suddenly, so I'd like us to be more consistent with our plans."	"I know we care about each other, and that makes me sure we can overcome this."
"I admire your patience with me, especially when I'm having a hard time."	"I've been feeling left out when decisions are made without me, and I'd appreciate us talking things through more."	"I'm in this for the long run and want to keep growing together, no matter what."
"I value how much you work to keep our relationship strong."	"It's tough when we don't communicate much, and I think checking in with each other more often would help."	"I trust we can handle this because we've faced tough times before and came out stronger."

Think of and describe something you need to talk about with your FP:

_____

_____

_____

Describe something you appreciate about your FP or your relationship (use something from the first column above or create your own):

_____

_____

_____

What's the tense or possible emotionally-activating issue? Describe what you'd like to change without making accusations or judgments about your FP; use something from the middle column or create your own:

_____

_____

_____

What's another positive statement showing you're committed to making things work to your FP? (Use something from the middle column or create your own.)

_____

_____

_____

Great job, you've created your sandwich. Review and practice it, using imagery to help you map out saying it and how you think it'll be perceived. Don't let your BPD catastrophize it; be as objective as you can. You may want to practice it with a healthy other or a mental health provider before broaching it with your FP. Let's continue strengthening your relationship with direct and assertive communication skills.

Building Clear Connection Through Better Communication

The next exercise will help you build insight, manage BPD better, and improve your communication. The first part will teach you that not everything needs to be talked about right away, , waiting for the right moment can make a conversation more meaningful and less triggering. The next section will teach you how to avoid emotionally charged talks that can get off track, we call this derailment.

Take your time with these sections and think about your own experiences. You'll reflect on past situations and how using different approaches could have changed the outcome and lessened the adverse consequences of your BPD relationship problem areas being activated. These sections are meant to help you build better communication habits, so approach them openly. When writing your reflections, focus on what you've learned so far and how you can use that in future conversations. Remember, this is about progress, not perfection, every step brings you closer to stronger, empowered relationships.

TIMING OVER URGENCY

Before we dive in, let's take a look at how Paula gained control of her timing over urgency.

Paula often felt a strong urge to talk to Leon the moment he got home from his long workdays. Her BPD made her feel she had to address her feelings immediately, or they'd overwhelm her. This urgency, driven by fear of abandonment and rejection, left her feeling out of control, with her emotions running the show. Rushing into conversations with intensity often led to arguments, leaving them both hurt and distant.

Through insight and practice, Paula learned that pausing to breathe and process her emotions before speaking made a big difference. She began by appreciating Leon's hard work, calmly sharing her feelings, and ending with reassurance. By waiting for the right moment and not letting BPD take over, their conversations became more productive. This shift helped Paula avoid triggering her relationship problem areas, improving communication and building a stronger, closer relationship.

This following exercise helped Paula understand why she felt the need to jump into tough, emotionally charged conversations right away, which increased the probability of getting into an argument. Before you dive in, think about a time when you felt the urge to start a conversation right away, like it just couldn't wait.

Describe the issue and what made it so urgent.

_____

_____

_____

_____

What emotions, thoughts, and images were you experiencing and how did they affect you?

_____

_____

_____

Who was in control, BPD or you? Describe how you know this.

_____

_____

_____

Describe what happened when you jumped into the conversation right away.

_____

_____

_____

How did this amplify your BPD relationship problem areas?

_____

_____

_____

What might have been different if you'd waited before jumping into the conversation?

_____

_____

_____

What do you wish you would've done differently?

_____

_____

_____

URGENCY REDO:

Before jumping into your next tough conversation, use the insight you gained from the previous prompts and pair it with the steps below:

1. Pause and remind yourself that being in control means staying in the moment, not stuck in thoughts about the past or future.

2. Pay attention to your body. Start from your head and slowly notice how your body feels, where you're comfortable, and where you feel tense.

3. Think about what's going through your mind. What thoughts or images are there?

4. Ask yourself, is this really the best time for both of us to talk about this?

5. Think about whether it would help if you both took some time to calm down or think things through first.

These five steps, along with your insight, will help you take control and stop your BPD from pushing you to act right away, or yell and demand immediate attention to the issue out of fear of losing everything. Try using the sandwich technique with these steps and your insight, which supercharges you with control. To further enhance this, we have to help you stay on track and avoid conversation derailment, which we'll go over now.

DETERING DERAILMENT

Conversation derailment happens when a discussion goes off track, becomes hurtful, and amplifies BPD relationship issues. It can happen when someone changes the subject, dismisses the other person, name-calls, makes assumptions, or avoids the real issue by focusing on how things are said instead of what's being said.

In texts or online chats, this often leads to personal attacks, diverting attention from the main topic. Sometimes, people derail conversations to avoid responsibility or question motives to dodge the real problem. It might feel like you're protecting yourself from rejection or abandonment, but it worsens BPD issues and deepens feelings of emptiness.

The following exercise will help you stay on track in conversations, especially when emotions run high, and manage BPD's adverse impact. Before starting, check out how Paula handled Leon's tendency to derail conversations.

Paula felt anxious because Leon was working so much, and her BPD made her fear he was pulling away. Determined to stay calm, she used the sandwich technique and managed her urgency when talking to him. As the conversation went on, Leon started talking about unrelated topics. Paula noticed the conversation derailment but stayed calm and gently brought it back on track, reminding Leon their focus was on spending more time together.

By managing her BPD and emotions, Paula kept the conversation from spiraling into an argument. Staying focused and not letting her fears take over helped her feel more in control and closer to Leon, while keeping her BPD relationship issues in check.

You can handle instances of derailment just like Paula by using the skills you've learned and the ones you're about to learn. The exercise below will help you keep your conversations on track, using strategies that focus on healthy resolution and managing your BPD relationship problems.

First, identify those things that may cause the conversation to go off track (consider your top three BPD relationship problem areas).

List your top three BPD relationship problem areas below:

1. _____

2. _____

3. _____

What are some things that usually cause your conversations to go off track and how are they related to your BPD relationship problem areas?

_____

_____

_____

_____

_____

_____

What can you do to stay focused on the main issue without getting sidetracked? For example, if you feel a sudden urge to accuse your partner of abandonment or start overreacting to something, take a deep breath and remind yourself to stay focused on the main issue you want to discuss.

_____

_____

_____

_____

Describe what you can do if the conversation gets off track. For example, gently remind your partner, "Remember, we're trying to find a solution that makes us both feel better about our relationship."

_____

_____

_____

_____

Reflect on the conversation. How did it go or how do you imagine it going? Write down what worked, and what you can do differently next time. For example, you might write, "The conversation went well because I stayed calm, but next time I need to focus more on listening without interrupting."

_____

_____

_____

_____

Using these strategies and paying attention to your emotions and communication goals can really help you feel more understood. But remember, your BPD might make you feel uncomfortable or resist this change. Even though change can be scary, it's worth it. The more you manage your BPD, the less it will hurt your relationships. Good communication is key to building strong connections. By focusing on timing, staying positive, being clear about your needs, and keeping conversations on track, you can strengthen your relationships. Just remember, good communication takes practice, so keep trying!

Setting the Stage for Relationship Success

Using the spaces below, pull together what you learned from this chapter so you can take this information with you and use it in your relationships.

How will the skills you've learned in this chapter help you manage your top three BPD relationship problem areas?

_____

_____

_____

_____

In what ways can the skills you've learned in this chapter help you respond more calmly to disagreements or feedback?

_____

_____

_____

_____

What skills can you apply from this chapter to have greater mood stabilization and maintain consistency in your relationship?

_____

_____

_____

_____

What can you use from this chapter to build a close relationship with your FP?

_____

_____

_____

_____

How can the skills you've learned in this chapter help you increase trust, acceptance, and love in your relationship?

_____

_____

_____

_____

By working through intimacy challenges in this chapter, you've learned to communicate better, express your needs authentically, and build a deeper connection with your FP. These are important steps toward healthier relationships, but the journey isn't over. Many of your relationship struggles come from old patterns and beliefs that BPD amplifies and keeps alive.

Next, we'll explore these destructive patterns and how they affect your current relationships. By recognizing and challenging them, you can rewrite the story they tell about you and your connections, creating space for healthier, more balanced relationships moving forward.

CHAPTER 8

Breaking and Replacing Old Destructive Patterns

You're doing great at staying strong and managing how BPD affects your relationship with your FP. In this chapter, you'll learn about something that shapes how you see yourself, others, and your world: internalized patterns. These are habits and beliefs from past experiences that still impact your relationships now. When BPD controls these habits, it tricks you into thinking they're helpful, but they often make your fears more likely to come true.

For example, if you feel hurt or ignored by your FP, you might try to get back at them or pull away. It might feel right at the moment, but it often leaves you feeling guilty or ashamed. Even if it doesn't work, BPD convinces you to try again, trapping you in a harmful cycle. Learning to notice these habits and pausing before reacting helps you make better choices for the healthy relationship you want.

The second part of this chapter will help you see how old patterns and BPD tendencies affect your view of your FP. It's about challenging distorted views and letting go of unrealistic expectations. By doing this, you create space for a healthier, more balanced relationship where both of you feel seen for who you truly are, not through the lens of past fears or BPD needs.

By the end of this chapter, you'll have tools to break those harmful patterns and build stronger, more meaningful connections. Let's start by looking at Kyle and his relationship with Melissa.

• Kyle and Melissa

Kyle grew up with parents who barely paid attention to him and rarely showed interest or support. They never set rules, leaving him feeling lost and unsure of what was okay. Without guidance, he struggled to understand himself, and life felt unpredictable and scary. At school, rules were confusing, making him feel like everything was working against him. His parents mostly criticized him, making him feel unimportant and convincing him he had to work hard for anyone to care.

As Kyle got older, these experiences shaped how he saw himself and others, especially in relationships. Diagnosed with BPD at 23, he finally understood why his emotions were so intense and why his relationships were chaotic. He constantly feared abandonment, struggled to trust others, and overreacted when he felt uncared for. Even when things were going well, he doubted their stability, creating ongoing BPD relationship problems.

When Kyle met Melissa in a cooking class, he felt hopeful. Melissa was kind and confident, and for a while, being with her made him feel safe. But soon, his BPD issues surfaced. Kyle became intensely jealous and worried Melissa would leave him. He tested her loyalty, sometimes pushing her away just to see if she'd come back. Even when Melissa needed space or gently offered feedback, Kyle saw it as betrayal, triggering anxiety and anger.

Kyle's fear of abandonment and need for control began straining their relationship. He realized that if he didn't address his BPD patterns, he could lose Melissa, the very thing he feared most. Determined to change, Kyle decided to work on managing his emotions and building healthier relationships.

You may relate to Kyle's experiences and struggles with BPD and those internalized patterns that felt like they were built into his DNA, but they're not. To change them, he had to uncover them first, just like you're about to do.

Identifying My Internalized Patterns

Your views and reactions to yourself, others, your FP, and relationships are shaped by "internal patterns" developed from past experiences, especially with important people like parents or caregivers. These patterns formed because similar experiences kept happening, teaching you what to expect and how to respond. They still influence your behavior today, especially with those who matter most, like your FP.

These internalized patterns run beneath the surface, triggering reactions almost automatically, like a reflex. It's similar to how your leg kicks out when a doctor taps your knee; it happens without thinking. BPD can make these "reflexive patterns" feel like they control your emotions and behaviors, leading to frustration, insecurity, and relationship barriers.

Unlike a real reflex, these patterns aren't automatic biological responses. They're learned reactions meant to protect you. But, like any skill, you can learn to recognize and change these patterns from unhealthy to healthy. While you can't control a real knee-jerk reflex, you can control your knee-jerk reactions influenced by internalized patterns.

These patterns, amplified by BPD, can make relationships feel like they only heighten fear and emotional sensitivity, pulling you deeper into despair. Without intending to, you often react in ways that push people away, even though you crave connection and closeness. The good news? Once you recognize these patterns, you can start changing them, rewriting your rule book to build healthier, more positive relationships moving forward.

Discovering Your Internalized Patterns

Uncovering your internalized patterns will help you see how your early experiences with your parents or caregivers affect the way you see yourself, others, and relationships today. The exercise below is going to help you figure this out. You're going to start by reflecting on the important relationships you had while growing up. Try not to see people or relationships as either all good or all bad (resist splitting). It's not about them being perfect, evil, or completely ignoring you; instead, focus on the overall patterns of behavior and response, or lack of it. This will help you understand how your early experiences shaped the way you trust and connect with people today.

Understanding this part of yourself can help you build healthier connections with others, just like it did for Kyle.

By completing the exercise below, Kyle gained valuable insight into how his early relationships shaped the way he behaves in his current relationships, especially with Melissa, his FP. Reflecting on the issues helped Kyle realize that his feelings of being ignored and unimportant carried over into his adult relationships, causing him to seek constant reassurance and fear abandonment.

The exercise allowed Kyle to connect these past experiences to the patterns he follows now, such as feeling anxious when Melissa needed space or testing her loyalty. By becoming aware of these patterns and how they affect his emotions, Kyle was able to pause before reacting, giving him the chance to choose healthier responses. This awareness helped Kyle create more stability and trust in his relationship, breaking the cycle of insecurity and improving his emotional well-being.

PATTERNS FROM THE PAST

Describe your important relationships with people growing up (such as parents, caregivers, or close family).

_____

_____

_____

_____

_____

What issues or problems did you have with the people you listed above (if you felt ignored by someone listed, do you now feel anxious when your partner doesn't respond quickly)?

_____

_____

_____

How do these issues from your past relationship show up in your current relationship with your FP (if you struggled with trust in a past relationship, do you find yourself feeling suspicious or needing constant reassurance from your FP now)?

_____

_____

_____

_____

List any thoughts, fears, or images you have when things don't go as expected with your FP and describe how you usually react in those moments (e.g., withdrawing, sending many texts, or shutting down emotionally).

_____

_____

_____

When the above occurs, what behaviors or patterns do you notice repeating (consider whether you tend to trust others easily or often find yourself seeking reassurance)?

_____

_____

_____

Let's link your past issues with the three problem areas in your relationships. To do this, reflect on how your internal patterns may contribute to or intensify these challenges. Consider where these patterns originated and how they affect your responses.

Problem Area #1: _____

_____

How the Pattern Affects This Area: _____

_____

Problem Area #2: _____

_____

How the Pattern Affects This Area: _____

_____

Problem Area #3: _____

_____

How the Pattern Affects This Area: _____

_____

Consider how engaging in your internalized patterns impacts your emotions. After you've acted on your patterns, consider how you feel about yourself, your FP, and the situation as a whole. For example, after seeking reassurance, you might feel frustrated with yourself for constantly needing validation, upset with your FP for not responding as quickly as you hoped, or overwhelmed by the entire situation. Before you complete your own, review Kyle's answers to guide you in reflecting on your patterns and feelings. You can use extra paper if you'd like to complete more than one of the exercises below, or you can download a copy of this exercise at http://www.newharbinger.com/56050.

When I act on my pattern, I feel **insecure** because **I'm afraid Melissa will leave me if I don't get constant reassurance,** and regarding my FP, I feel **frustrated** with my FP because **she doesn't always respond in the way I expect or quickly enough.** The whole situation makes me feel **overwhelmed and anxious, as if I need to do something drastic to keep her close.**

When I act on my pattern, I feel _____ because _____

_____,

and regarding my FP, I feel_____ because _____

_____.

The whole situation makes me feel _____

_____.

This exercise was to help you see how your usual habits affect your feelings, your thoughts about your FP, and your relationship overall. For example, Kyle noticed that when he looks for reassurance, he feels insecure and worries his FP might leave him. He also gets frustrated if his FP doesn't reply quickly, which leaves him feeling anxious and overwhelmed. Recognizing these patterns is a big step, but now it's time to understand why you fall into them and start changing them.

Urges and Your Old Patterns

You might feel like you have to follow certain habits or patterns to avoid feeling anxious, scared, lonely, or rejected. These responses can feel automatic, but you have more control than you think. Recognizing your patterns is a big first step. Now, it's about managing the urges that keep you stuck. Your internalized patterns stick around because they feel familiar, not because they're healthy. These urges feel like quick reflexes, convincing you that acting this way will protect you from hurt or abandonment. But instead of helping, they keep you trapped in the same problems, making BPD and relationship issues worse.

Old patterns give BPD a lot of control over how you think, feel, and view your relationships. Breaking free starts with noticing the urge to react in the same old ways, like seeking reassurance or lashing out. When these urges come up, pause. That pause gives you the power to choose a healthier response. It's not easy, but it's worth it. Practicing this pause will weaken the hold of your BPD patterns, helping you build better habits and relationships. The key is recognizing and controlling the urge before it pulls you back into those old, harmful patterns.

Let's take a look at Kyle's urges and experience with this before you dive into the exercise.

Kyle sat at the kitchen table, staring at his phone. Melissa hadn't replied in over 5 minutes, and the urge to text her again was building fast. His thoughts spiraled, Is she mad? Is she pulling away? The anxiety grew, and he felt the familiar need to fix it by reaching out again, thinking it would calm him down. But Kyle knew this was his old pattern, seeking continual reassurance, and that it never really helped in the end. He paused. He had learned about how his BPD fueled these fears of abandonment, making his emotions feel out of control. He realized that texting Melissa wouldn't ease his anxiety in the long run, it would just reinforce his insecurities. Instead, Kyle took a deep breath and sat with the discomfort, noticing the racing thoughts and tension. He chose not to text, creating space between the urge and his reaction. This pause gave him clarity, reminding him that his urge came from BPD, not reality. Over time, this strategy helped him build trust and security in his relationship with Melissa, free from the old habits that used to weigh him down.

Take Control of Your Urges and Patterns

Before you begin this exercise, take a moment to consider why it's important. This exercise is designed to help you notice when your urges come up, understand what's driving them, and provide you with deeper insight into your urges and actions. By taking the time to pause, reflect, and choose a different path, you can begin to break free from old patterns and make healthier choices. This isn't about being perfect; it's about learning to pause and make thoughtful decisions, one step at a time.

Take your time with each step, and remember, the more you practice, the more control you'll gain over your responses.

Below, you're going to be asked to list your top three relationship problem areas and the urges that come with them. If you'd like additional examples, please visit http://www.newharbinger.com/56050.

Top Three Relationship Problem Areas	Urges (Thoughts, Fears, or Images)

We're going to break down your urge and associated features into thoughts, feelings, and images to build insight. To get started, describe what thoughts, feelings, and images are fueling your urges associated with your top three relationship problem areas.

Thoughts (example: *If I don't reach out, they might be angry, and I'll lose them.*):

_____

_____

_____

Feelings (example: *I feel scared, anxious, and worried.*):

_____

_____

_____

Images (example: *I imagine them ignoring me forever or telling me they don't care.*):

_____

_____

_____

What do you believe will happen if you follow through using your old, internalized patterns (example: *If I send the text, I'll feel better because I'll know they're not mad.*)?:

_____

_____

_____

How do you expect to feel afterward (example: *I think I'll feel relieved... but only for a little while, until she gets upset again and I need more reassurance.*)?:

_____

_____

_____

How does your BPD influence your urges (e.g., *It makes me feel like if I don't get reassurance right now, I'll be abandoned.*)?:

_____

_____

_____

What did you learn about your BPD and your urges (example: *I realized that the urge doesn't last forever. It passes if I give it time. My BPD is tricking me*).

_____

_____

_____

Pick one or more of the following strategies to try when your urge hits and BPD starts its games in your mind.

The Three-Breath Rule:

- Take three slow, deep breaths before doing anything. This creates a small gap where you can think more clearly.

Curiosity Break:

- Ask yourself: *What's really happening here?* Instead of acting on the urge, become curious about it. What's it trying to do? What's the deeper feeling behind it?

Disrupt the Pattern:

- Get up and move, walk, stretch, or do something physical to shake off the automatic response.

Reality Check:

- Ask yourself: *What's the actual evidence that this situation is as bad as I think?* Write down what's real versus what your emotions are exaggerating.

Shift to Values:

- Think about what matters most to you at this moment. What action would honor your values, like trust, patience, or self-respect, instead of reacting out of fear?

After you've tried one of the strategies, take a moment to reflect.

How did it feel to do something different instead of reflexively responding (example: *It was hard at first, but I felt more in control.*)?:

_____

_____

_____

_____

_____

How can you use this next time (e.g., *I'll remind myself that I don't have to react right away and that taking a breath gives me space to choose*)?:

_____

_____

_____

_____

_____

Now that you've learned how to recognize and manage your pattern urges, let's take it a step further. We're going to focus on how pausing and using one of the strategies listed above and not reacting right away gives you a chance to see yourself and others differently and provides you an opportunity to react in another way, increasing the likelihood of creating a new adaptive pattern. This *pause and consider* approach creates space for healthier, more positive responses that can break old patterns. Over time, this approach will help you form new patterns that strengthen your relationships and boost your emotional well-being.

Building Better Habits for Healthier Responses

Next, you'll be building on the insights and skills you've gained about your BPD patterns and strengthening the healthy strategies you've learned throughout the workbook. This part of the chapter is going to help you take steps toward change by practicing new habits that put you back in control of your emotions and reactions. This exercise will help you reduce the level of intense urgency, build more trust with your FP, and express yourself in a way that brings you closer to the people who matter most. These new habits will lead to better communication, more emotional balance, and a deeper, more fulfilling connection in your relationships. You've already made so much progress, now it's time to keep going and see the benefits in your everyday life.

Building Healthy Responses for Growth and Connection

In this next exercise, you're going to work on self-reflection and growth, exploring how you see yourself and ways to build better relationships. To start, you're going to identify those limiting or empowering beliefs. Limiting beliefs are negative thoughts like, *I'm not good enough*, or *I always pick the wrong person*, often rooted in past bad experiences, which can hold you back and keep you stuck in unhealthy patterns. Empowering beliefs, like *I deserve love*, or *I can learn from my past*, help boost your confidence, set healthy boundaries, and guide you to make better choices. By replacing limiting beliefs with empowering ones, you can build stronger relationships and create a path toward positive change.

Each step through this exercise will guide you to explore your self-worth, let go of old habits, and create healthier emotional responses. By the end, you'll have access to the tools for emotional resilience and deeper connections with others. Through reflection, writing, and setting goals, you'll create a path toward positive change beyond your BPD. I've added some of Kyle's responses as examples to help you get started.

What beliefs do you hold about who you are, and are these beliefs limiting or empowering?

_____

_____

_____

Circle which one applies most: **Limiting**   **Empowering**

Do you see yourself as deserving of love, care, and respect?   **Yes**   **No**

Look at yourself beyond your BPD lens and influence, and elaborate on your previous answer:

_____

_____

_____

Write 3 affirmations about your worth and 3 goals for personal and relational growth (e.g., *I am worthy of love and respect. I will trust myself to handle emotional challenges without needing constant reassurance*).

_____

_____

_____

What past internalized beliefs, behaviors, and patterns work against your affirmations of worth (e.g., *I believed I had to have attention to be worthy of love, which made it hard to accept my worth. This fear of abandonment led me to jealousy and pushing people away*)?

_____

_____

_____

Use the questions below to outline how you can incorporate the three letting go strategies of old patterns to encourage future growth potential for you and your relationship.

Commit to letting go of the past (e.g., *I've decided to stop letting my childhood control my relationships. I write down memories to release and use a daily affirmation to stay focused on the present*).

_____

_____

_____

Identify your emotional patterns (e.g., *I reflect on my past relationship patterns of jealousy and fear of abandonment, then track these emotions in a journal to identify triggers*).

_____

_____

_____

Train your mind for empowered thinking (e.g., *I replace negative thoughts with positive ones by pausing, breathing, and repeating affirmations like* I am worthy of love and stability *to train my mind*).

_____

_____

_____

Let's help you reorient your thinking to influence your emotions and patterns. What new coping strategies can you use to manage emotions and build resilience (e.g., *I'll pause when anxious, focus on my breathing, and remind myself I don't need constant reassurance. I'll practice open communication instead of assuming the worst*)?

_____

_____

_____

Identify at least two of the following empowering daily habits you can do to help you stay mindful and present:

☐ Regular meditation

☐ Mindful breathing exercises

☐ Journaling my thoughts

☐ Identifying triggers

☐ Replacing negative self-talk with positive affirmations

☐ Practicing gratitude

☐ Engaging in physical activity

☐ Seeking support from a therapist when needed

☐ Focusing on being present in the moment

☐ Acknowledging my thoughts without judgment

Describe how you'll incorporate these new adaptive patterns into your daily routine so you're ready when your emotional urges arise (*I'll start each day by listing three things I'm grateful for to shift my mindset. When I feel anxious, I'll pause, breathe, and focus on the present to stay grounded*).

_____

_____

_____

Let's focus on integration. Describe how you can express your emotions and needs in a way that encourages connection and understanding (*I'll use "I" statements, like "I feel worried when...," to avoid blame and clearly express my needs, like asking for reassurance or space. I'll stay calm and listen to Melissa's feelings to ensure we both feel heard, fostering better understanding and connection).*

Write a script for an open, assertive conversation where you express your needs in a balanced way. (*I'd like to talk about how I feel when I'm anxious. I want us to find ways to support each other without falling into old patterns*).

After completing the exercise, take time to reflect on what you've learned about your self-perception, past patterns, and the new healthy responses you're building.

Describe how you feel about the steps you've taken toward personal growth and improving your relationship.

Detail how and when you'll continue practicing these strategies moving forward.

By completing this exercise, you've gained deeper insight into your self-perception, uncovered patterns from the past, and developed healthier ways to respond to emotional challenges. By actively practicing these new strategies, you're on the path to building stronger, more balanced relationships and fostering emotional resilience. Keep applying what you've learned, and trust that with each step, you're moving closer to lasting positive change in your life and relationships.

In this chapter, you've learned to spot and replace destructive patterns shaped by BPD. By identifying the internalized habits that drive your emotions and reactions, you can make conscious choices that support healthier relationships. Like Kyle, you can break free from limiting cycles, create space for understanding, and build deeper connections. Practicing these new strategies will strengthen your resilience and emotional balance, helping you grow both personally and in your relationships. Keep going, you're making real progress.

Setting the Stage for Relationship Success

Using the spaces below, pull together what you learned from this chapter so you can take this information with you and use it in your relationships.

How will the skills you've learned in this chapter help you manage your top three BPD relationship problem areas?

_____

_____

_____

_____

In what ways can the skills you've learned in this chapter help you respond more calmly to disagreements or feedback?

_____

_____

_____

_____

What skills can you apply from this chapter to have greater mood stabilization and maintain consistency in your relationship?

_____

_____

_____

_____

_____

What can you use from this chapter to build a close relationship with your FP?

_____

_____

_____

How can the skills you've learned in this chapter help you increase trust, acceptance, and love in your relationship?

_____

_____

_____

_____

It's time to take all the skills you've learned and built and use them to remap your relationship with your FP. This final chapter is all about celebrating your progress and internalizing those new, healthier ways of connecting. This next chapter will also help you recognize the changes you've already made to build a stronger, more trusting bond moving forward. Let's dive in and keep building on your great progress!

CHAPTER 9

From Struggle to Stability: Bringing It All Together

You've made amazing progress! Throughout this workbook, you've uncovered how BPD affects you and your relationships, especially with your FP. You've learned how to handle intense emotions, fears of abandonment, rejection, emptiness, mood swings, relationship problem areas, and set healthy boundaries. Now, as you put all these skills together, it's time to take one last step, remapping your relationship with your FP. This remapping journey is all about recognizing how far you've come and celebrating each small step and minimizing BPD's adverse impact. Just like learning any new skill, changes can feel challenging at first, but each small achievement moves you closer to a stronger, healthier relationship. Let's start by reflecting on your growth, but let's take a look at Tonya's challenges, barriers, and tenacity to overcome her BPD and emotional turmoil before diving in.

• Tonya's Triumph Over Turmoil

Tonya deeply wanted closeness with the people in her life, especially her FP, David. But her urges often got in the way. She struggled with feeling clingy, needing constant contact with David to feel secure. If he didn't reply quickly or seemed busy, she'd worry he didn't care, leading her to "test" the relationship, ignoring him or asking questions to see if he'd prove he cared. This often caused arguments and misunderstandings.

Their pattern of breaking up and making up became a cycle. Though painful, it felt like a temporary reset button for their relationship. But Tonya didn't want to keep repeating the same mistakes, so she started working on her reactions. Using new strategies, Tonya reminded herself of positive moments with David whenever her worries surfaced, recognizing her fears were often just emotions, not facts. She began challenging her "BPD lens," which often made her see situations negatively. Talking openly with David helped, and they agreed to check in regularly, giving her a sense of security without needing to test the relationship.

Over time, Tonya felt their connection grow stronger and more stable. She even wrote a reminder: "Relationships are stronger than one moment." Step by step, Tonya was learning to manage her emotions and build a trusting, secure relationship with David.

BPD Influences and Celebrating Progress

Reflecting on your relationship, like Tonya did, with the insights and skills you've learned will help you see how far you've come. Where BPD once caused intense fears or conflicts, amplifying your relationship problem areas, your adaptive skills, like calmly expressing needs and setting boundaries, have replaced reactive maladaptive habits. These changes boost your confidence and strengthen your connection with your FP. As you continue, each positive step reinforces trust and resilience, creating a solid foundation for a healthier, lasting relationship.

Reflect and Recognize: Seeing the Journey Without a BPD Lens

In this exercise, you're going to reflect on your past and present relationship patterns, specifically focusing on the dynamics between you and your FP. The goal is to help you observe how your initial BPD tendencies influenced the relationship. By comparing your past responses to the new, adaptive patterns you've developed through this workbook, you can recognize your progress and continue building healthier, more balanced relationship skills. By completing this exercise, you'll gain a deeper understanding of how far you've come in managing BPD tendencies and improving your relationship dynamics. Use this reflection as a foundation for continued growth and positive change.

Describe how your initial BPD tendencies (impulsivity, fear of abandonment, rejection, emptiness, mood swings and so on) impacted your relationship with your FP.

How has your perception of your FP and your relationship changed using the skills you learned from the workbook?

_____

_____

_____

What new patterns have you developed to respond to your FP's behaviors without triggering BPD-driven responses?

_____

_____

_____

Write down three common scenarios. These may include your relationship problem areas when you typically feel emotionally reactive or challenged, such as receiving unexpected criticism, when your FP doesn't respond immediately, or during a disagreement with a partner.

1. _____

_____

2. _____

_____

3. _____

_____

For each scenario, recall and write down how you would have responded in the past, especially when BPD-driven thoughts and behaviors were more active, such as intrusive thoughts (_They don't care about me_ or _I'm unworthy of love_), emotional urges (e.g., anger, shame, or fear of abandonment), and old maladaptive patterns (e.g., withdrawing, arguing, or seeking constant reassurance).

1. _____

_____

2. _____

_____

3. _____

_____

For each scenario, describe the adaptive skills and insights you've developed recently. For example, instead of withdrawing or reacting harshly when feeling ignored, take a moment to assess and communicate feelings calmly; rather than hinting at insecurity, directly say, "I feel anxious about our relationship right now." Share the need for personal space when stressed, ensuring both feel secure without over-relying on each other.

1. _____

_____

2. _____

_____

3. _____

_____

To help you see how far you've come and reinforce the behaviors that are working, list your old patterns on one side and your new skills on the other.

Old Maladaptive Patterns	New Adaptive Patterns

Maintaining Your Foundation of Stability with Your FP

In this section, you'll be asked to establish practices that promote consistency, open communication, and stability in your relationship with your FP. These exercises are designed to help you build healthy habits together, fostering trust and connection while reducing the influence of BPD tendencies like fear of abandonment, impulsivity, and intense emotional reactions. Let's get started.

Establish a regular check-in with your FP to maintain open communication. Like Tonya and David, who meet on Wednesdays at 7:00 p.m. after dinner, choose a weekly or monthly time that works for you both. Add it to your calendar to ensure you have a dedicated, predictable space to discuss feelings and strengthen understanding in your relationship.

Identify at least three stability practices you and your FP can do together, for example, take a relaxing walk each Sunday morning to connect in a peaceful environment or watch a movie together every Friday, or saying something kind daily (there is a list of more options at the end of the chapter to help).

1. _____

2. _____

3. _____

You've taken important steps by recognizing and practicing positive reinforcement techniques. BPD wants you to fall into old patterns of your negative thinking, fear of abandonment, or intense emotional reactions in relationships. The next section is going to help you get even closer in a healthy way using affirming statements and expressing gratitude, and by doing this you're challenging those once BPD ingrained beliefs and behaviors. It's not easy to push back against the urge to focus on what's wrong or feel overwhelmed by fears. However, each time you choose to notice the good and nurture those small moments of connection, you're actively working to lessen the impact of BPD relationship problems.

AFFIRMING STATEMENTS AND GRATITUDE FOR SMALL GESTURES

Think back over the past week and consider your recent interactions with your FP. Write down three small gestures they made that help you feel appreciated. For each gesture, include an affirming statement you could use to express your gratitude. Here are some examples from Tonya's worksheet, Gesture: *David took the time to listen when I was feeling upset.* Affirming Statement: *I really appreciate how patient you were with me today. It helped me feel heard and supported.*

Now it's your turn:

Gesture:_____

Affirming Statement: _____

Gesture: _____

Affirming Statement: _____

Gesture: _____

Affirming Statement: _____

A relationship wins journal can really help you keep your focus on the positives. This is a great way to track moments when those relationship victories emerge. You can also use this when BPD resurges, or you feel stuck in relationship turmoil. This journal includes times when you felt particularly connected, when communication went well, or when you noticed a positive change in behavior from yourself or your FP (e.g., *David and I had a really open conversation without arguing. I felt truly heard and validated, and I'm proud that I stayed calm even when I started to feel triggered*). There are two journal entry spaces below, but you can access more at http://www.newharbinger.com/56050.

Your Journal Entry:

Date: _____

Win: _____

Your Journal Entry:

Date: _____

Win: _____

Next, you're going to further strengthen your ability to identify the things that set off strong emotions, memories, thoughts, and images (your "buttons") in your relationship with your FP. By noticing these patterns, you can continue to break down old habits and make room for positive changes. Let's dive in to help you respond in a more controlled way to build a healthier relationship!

To complete this activity, you'll start by identifying a specific trigger or emotional button with your FP, something they do (or don't do) that sets off strong feelings. Then, identify the fear behind the trigger (e.g., fear of abandonment or rejection). Next, describe your immediate reaction, like what you say or do in the heat of the moment. Finally, look at the bigger pattern of behavior that keeps repeating over time. Understanding these four parts—trigger/button, fear, reaction, and pattern—will help you see the cycle more clearly and start breaking old habits to create healthier responses. To help, check out Tonya and David's example before you outline your own.

Trigger (Emotional Button): I feel upset when David doesn't respond to my messages quickly.

My Fear: I'm scared that he's ignoring me or that he might not love me anymore.

My Reaction: I send him multiple messages, asking if he's mad at me or if I did something wrong.

My Pattern: I often accuse David of not caring about me or being distant, even when he's just busy or unavailable.

Trigger (Emotional Button): _____

_____

My Fear: _____

_____

My Reaction: _____

_____

My Pattern: _____

_____

_____

Trigger (Emotional Button): _____

_____

My Fear: _____

_____

My Reaction: _____

_____

My Pattern: _____

_____

_____

Turning Setbacks into Stepping Stones

Growth and change take time and it's not a linear process, meaning it's not always forward movement. There will be times when you slide backward, but you don't go all the way back to zero or start, you go back a few steps and then realign and continue forward. You've made it this far in this workbook, a true testament to your tenacity and strength. Let's embrace the insight and skills you learned and further prepare you for those intensive expectations, insecurities, and possible regressions.

It's understandable to feel overwhelmed sometimes, within your relationship and when outside of it. Instead of getting stuck in your negative cycle that pulls you back into your BPD relationship problem areas, you can use the tools you've learned to help ground yourself in the present, where you're most powerful and in control. In the following exercise, you'll create a grounding statement—a simple phrase to help you calm down and remind you it's okay to struggle. It might feel strange at first, but the more you practice, the easier it'll be to internalize kind words. Remember, setbacks are expected, and using your grounding statement is a positive step forward in building your sense of self and lessening the intensity of negative thoughts and feelings.

Retaining Control During Regression

You're going to start by writing down one or two common negative thoughts you have when you're overwhelmed, like *I'm unlovable* or *I've messed everything up*. Then, create a kind response, like, *It's okay to struggle; I'm still making progress.* Practice using these grounding statements when you're stressed, focusing on your breath. They really are powerful. Finally, you're going to write them down on a small card or save them on your phone for a quick reminder whenever you need them.

Write down one or two common negative thoughts you have when you're feeling overwhelmed, especially the ones that come up during tough moments with your FP and tend to trigger regressions back to those BPD maladaptive beliefs, behaviors, and patterns (e.g., *I'm a burden, and they'll leave because I'm too much*).

_____

_____

_____

_____

Now, it's time to create your grounding statement—that kind, compassionate response to counter your negative thoughts. This should be something gentle, like what a supportive friend might say to comfort you. Write your grounding statement here (e.g., *It's okay to struggle; I'm still worthy of love. This moment doesn't define me, I'm learning, and I can handle this*).

_____

_____

_____

_____

_____

Reminder: Next time you feel overwhelmed, repeat your grounding statement slowly, focusing on your breath. Imagine each word bringing calm and comfort. Saying it out loud or even whispering can make it feel more real and soothing.

Where will you keep your grounding statement so it's easy to access when you need a quick reminder—on a small card, in your phone's notes app, or pinned somewhere you'll see it often? Use it as part of your daily routine, like reading it to yourself before bed or when you wake up. (*I'll save it in my phone's notes and write it on a card for my wallet, so it's always with me.*)

You've learned valuable skills to help you maintain control when you feel the flood of BPD beliefs, behaviors, and patterns that seem to pull you back to those relationship problem areas. Your arsenal of insight and adaptive techniques will help you stay present and handle intense emotions without losing control. It's time to shift your gears and embrace what's ahead.

The next section is going to help you further consolidate a plan for ongoing progress and encourage reflection and set positive intentions for your future. Instead of letting things just happen, you're taking charge by setting goals and creating a plan for what comes next. This helps you feel more in control, making decisions now that'll build a healthier, more balanced connection with your FP. You're choosing to work on the relationship you want, taking steps to grow and improve, and preparing for the challenges that might come your way.

Future Focused, Empowered, and in Control

To get to any destination, you need to know how to get there. Relationships are the same way. To achieve relationship success without BPD's adverse influence, you have to create a personal progress map. There are ten-mile markers on your road for you to list tough moments or behaviors you've managed to handle better since you've started your journey through this workbook, but don't stop there. Also include new skills or insights you've developed, like better communication or increased self-awareness, and add in words or quotes that inspire you and remind you of how far you've come. This is your journey, and although you're almost at the end of this workbook, you'll take it all with you.

1. _____

   _____

2. _____

   _____

3. _____

   _____

4. _____

_____

5. _____

_____

6. _____

_____

7. _____

_____

8. _____

_____

9. _____

_____

10. _____

_____

For this final step, you'll revisit your top three relationship problem areas and see just how much progress you've made. This step reinforces your ability to steer your path, choosing harmony over conflict and keeping the power in your hands.

Maintaining Your Power to Choose

BPD often draws you toward conflict, fueled by its maladaptive patterns and the challenging dynamics it fosters with your FP. But with awareness comes choice, the power to choose a path of harmony over discord. Use this moment to recognize how far you've come and to reaffirm your ability to take control of your journey, one decision at a time. Remember, harmony sets you up for a stronger, healthier relationship where both you and your FP can feel more secure and supported.

For your final exercise, you'll be asked to rate the degree of impact your relationship problem areas have on your relationship with your FP back then ("Then"), start of workbook, compared to now ("Now"). Rate each one from 0 (no impact at all) to 5 (severely affects the relationship, creates major disruptions and conflict). You'll then dive deeper, enhancing your insight and employing your adaptive strategies over those old BPD maladaptive ones.

0 = None (No impact at all)

1 = Very Low Impact (Barely noticeable, rarely affects the relationship)

2 = Low Impact (Occasionally noticed but manageable)

3 = Moderate Impact (Frequently noticed, sometimes causes tension)

4 = High Impact (Significantly affects the relationship, often leads to conflict)

5 = Highly Impactful (Severely affects the relationship, creates major disruptions and conflict)

Relationship Problem Area	Then	Now
1.		
2.		
3.		

Now that you've reassessed your top three relationship problem areas and noted your progress, let's go a little further. Choose *one* of the problem areas where you've seen the most improvement, and answer the following questions.

What actions or new strategies helped reduce the impact of this issue (reflect on the tools, exercises, or shifts in thinking that made the most difference)?

_____

_____

_____

What did you do differently, and how did it change the situation?

_____

_____

_____

_____

How can you maintain this progress moving forward (identify specific behaviors or reminders you can use to prevent slipping back into old patterns)?

_____

_____

_____

_____

What's one small step you can take today to foster harmony in your relationship? Choose a small, actionable way you can show your commitment to a healthier, more secure relationship with your FP. This could be practicing a grounding technique before a tough conversation, expressing appreciation, or setting a boundary with compassion.

_____

_____

_____

This exercise emphasizes your progress while also reinforcing the need to continue practicing the skills and strategies you've learned.

Congratulations on making it through this workbook! You've put in a lot of effort to better understand yourself, your FP, and the challenges you face together. It hasn't been easy, but you've done the hard work of recognizing and starting to overcome the unhelpful beliefs, behaviors, and patterns that BPD brings to your relationships. Remember, progress can feel slow at times but every step forward matters. You now have new tools, ideas, and insights to build a stronger, healthier connection. Keep practicing what you've learned, be patient and kind to yourself, and don't forget to celebrate the small victories along the way, as well as the big ones. Growth isn't about being perfect; it's about making small, positive changes that add up over time. With patience and commitment, you can create the loving, supportive relationship you deserve. You're on the right path, and you've got this!

If you need more help, I'll always be here in your workbook, ready to revisit and empower you. Be well, be strong, and embrace that knowledge is empowerment.

References

American Psychiatric Association. 2022. *Diagnostic and Statistical Manual of Mental Disorders* (5th ed., text rev.). Washington, DC: American Psychiatric Association.

Fox, D. J. 2019. *The Borderline Personality Disorder Workbook: An Integrative Program to Understand and Manage Your BPD.* New Harbinger Publications.

Fox, D. J. 2022. *Complex Borderline Personality Disorder: How Coexisting Conditions Affect Your BPD and How You Can Gain Emotional Balance.* New Harbinger Publications.

Gunderson, J. G., I. Weinberg, M. T. Daversa, K. D. Kueppenbender, M. C. Zanarini, and M. T. Shea, et al. 2006. "Descriptive and Longitudinal Observations on the Relationship of Borderline Personality Disorder and Bipolar Disorder." *American Journal of Psychiatry,* 163(7): 1173–1178.

MacMillan, C. 2019 "'The Father of BPD' John G. Gunderson, 1942–2019." *Journal of the American Academy of Child and Adolescent Psychiatry.* 58(5): 544–545. doi: 10.1016/j.jaac.2019.03.020. PMID: 31029199.

Shickler, S., and J. Waller. 2019. *The 7 Mindsets To Live Your Ultimate Life: An Unexpected Blueprint for an Extraordinary Life.* Publish Your Purpose.

Daniel J. Fox, PhD, is a licensed psychologist in Texas, international speaker, and multi-award-winning author. He has been specializing in the treatment and assessment of individuals with personality disorders for more than twenty years in the state and federal prison system, universities, and in private practice. Fox shares insights and treatment strategies for personality disorders and other forms of mental illness on his website and social media. His online content has been recognized as a valuable resource for both professionals and individuals seeking to understand and manage psychological conditions. Fox maintains a website and is on social media to present various treatment interventions focused on working with individuals along the antisocial, borderline, narcissistic, and histrionic personality spectrum.

MORE BOOKS from
NEW HARBINGER PUBLICATIONS

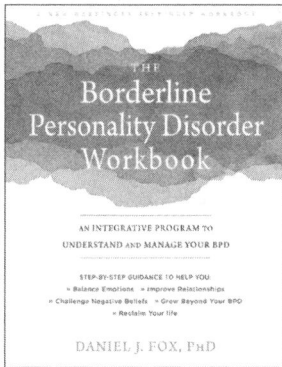

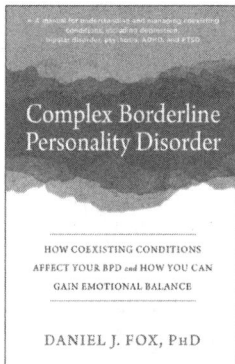

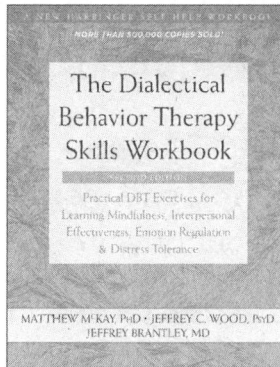

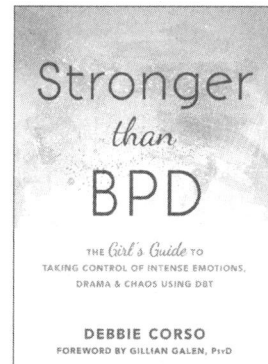

Did you know there are **free tools** you can download for this book?

Free tools are things like **worksheets**, **guided meditation exercises**, and **more** that will help you get the most out of your book.

You can download free tools for this book—whether you bought or borrowed it, in any format, from any source—from the New Harbinger website. All you need is a NewHarbinger.com account. Just use the URL provided in this book to view the free tools that are available for it. Then, click on the "download" button for the free tool you want, and follow the prompts that appear to log in to your NewHarbinger.com account and download the material.

You can also save the free tools for this book to your **Free Tools Library** so you can access them again anytime, just by logging in to your account! Just look for this button on the book's free tools page.

+ Save this to my free tools library

If you need help accessing or downloading free tools, visit **newharbinger.com/faq** or contact us at **customerservice@newharbinger.com**.